SPANISH ROUNDABOUT

Books by Maureen Daly

SEVENTEENTH SUMMER
SMARTER AND SMOOTHER
MY FAVORITE STORIES
THE PERFECT HOSTESS
WHAT'S YOUR P.Q.?
TWELVE AROUND THE WORLD
PATRICK VISITS THE FARM
SPANISH ROUNDABOUT

With William P. McGivern
MENTION MY NAME IN MOMBASA

SPANISH ROUNDABOUT

By Maureen Daly

ILLUSTRATED WITH PHOTOGRAPHS

Dodd, Mead & Company
New York

© by Maureen Daly, 1960
All rights reserved

No part of this book may be reproduced in any form without permission in writing from the publisher

The description of the girl in the first part of Chapter 6, *Teen-Aged Profiles—Señorita Y Señor*, first appeared under the title *Teen Ager—Spanish Style*, in the February 1959 issue of *American Girl* magazine, published by the Girl Scouts of the U.S.A. It is reprinted here with their gracious permission.

EIGHTH PRINTING

Library of Congress Catalog Card Number: 60-6309
Printed in the United States of America
by The Haddon Craftsmen, Inc., Scranton, Penna.

FOR MY DEAR FRIEND
Senora Pilar Pulgar-Peterson
OF MALAGA

Contents

1. Let's Take a Look — 1
2. A Cook's Tour — 15
3. Spanish Fiestas—Pageantry, Pinwheels and Prayers — 33
4. Spanish Customs: Black Bands to Bombas — 49
5. Famous Spaniards — 66
6. Teen-Aged Profiles—Señorita Y Señor — 86
7. Bravo! The Bulls! — 105
8. Snapshots in Spain — 126
9. Mosques, Moors—and Other Memories — 140
10. Diary Without Dates — 156
11. *Hasta Luego, Amigos* — 172
    Index — 175

Illustrations

Photographic supplement follows page 84

> Pictures through the courtesy of the Spanish Tourist Office

Here is a typical plaza, the heart of every village or big-city neighborhood. Cool shade for resting, a tinkling fountain—and old friends to chat with.

Soon these flooded rice paddies outside Valencia will sprout a brilliant green. Here a farm worker surf-boards over surface to cultivate rich, black soil. Horses as work-beasts are both expensive and rare.

An early morning catch is hauled from the Mediterranean outside Malaga. Fishing methods are centuries old and rough seas make work difficult. But men and boys toil side by side to eke out meager daily rations.

Solemnity and splendor spark this Holy Week procession in Seville. Each parish sends out its statue of the Virgin, jeweled and decked as the Queen of Heaven. Flower-trimmed floats number into the hundreds.

Triana celebrates a holiday—the "name day" of the town saint. Silken shawls draped from balconies are family treasures, brought out only for special occasions; straw blinds keep out hot sun, persistent flies.

Simple village street in southern Spain with rough, cobbled walks and white-washed houses. Barred windows keep out more cats than thieves. Inner courtyards make airy summer quarters, a-blaze with flowers.

Every day is wash-day in rural Spain. This matron in the central province of Leon is carrying a load to local stream. Roman ruins still stand nearby.

Sunlight, sand, brave matadors and applauding crowds. This is the great bullfight spectacle. Horses are thickly padded to prevent injury.

Modern farm equipment is rare in country Spain. Giant work cows, a special breed, pull wagons on rural roads, heads masked against the summer sun.

"Sounds of Christmas music" for sale in city market. Tambourines are made of goatskin and bits of tin; crown-topped *bombas* sound like big bullfrogs.

Flamenco, the gypsy-born dance of Spain, rings with sound, swirls with movement. Dancers stamp feet, clap hands to point up wild, staccato rhythms.

Illustrations - xi

At Cordoba, red and white striped arches fill the famed mosque-cathedral, a union of two religious architectures. Surrounding orange groves scent the air.

The tower, *La Giralda,* in Seville is built upon the remains of a Moorish mosque. Tower was built in 12th century, is famous for swinging brass bell.

These Gothic towers, pitted with time, have survived since Middle Ages. Modern Barcelona is a gay port city, little-sister to sophisticated Madrid.

At the graceful Court of the Lions in the Alhambra, 124 white marble columns support intricate fret-work arches constructed by old Moorish craftsmen.

The intersection of the Calle Alcala and the Cibeles Fountain in beautiful, busy Madrid. The Gran Via branches off to the right in the background.

Chapter I

LET'S TAKE A LOOK

W<small>HAT DO YOU</small> *see* when you look at Spain? Many things—some as old as crumbling Roman aqueducts, some as new as shiny, shark-nosed jets. Spain is not just one picture. It is a series of sharp, brilliant scenes played side by side, separate yet all part of the total spectacle of this great country.

For instance, *this* is a picture of Spain: at four o'clock one fall morning, we went down to the tiny fishing village of Carahuela to go out with a fishing crew. By the light of a clouded moon, we could make out the rows of whitewashed cottages lining the sandy beach streets and the pinnacle and bell tower of a little church. The only electric light burning was the single bulb hanging over the bar in a fishermen's cafe. Inside, the cafe owner dozed on a floor littered with shrimp shells, sand and short, blackened cigarette stubs. Outside, the waves of the Mediterranean made a muted, measured roar.

One by one, fishermen came into the cafe, rubbing whiskered, tired faces, some old, weather-beaten men, some boys of sixteen. The cafe owner set up breakfast on the bar—squares of bread and little glasses of sharp, strong anis. Two boats were to fish in a pair, with a crew of eight each, and we all huddled in the chill, dim bar until the men had gathered.

In the shadowy moonlight, the big rowboats were shoved into the rough water; the last of the crew hopped in just as the craft hit the waves. Sea spray soaked us all and the wind blew cold. The fishermen in their thin shirts and cotton pants seemed to shiver in rhythm, the same rhythm in which they rowed. For a silent hour, the crew pulled at the oars, keeping the craft side by side. Then the boats fanned out until they were about five hundred yards apart. The oarsmen sang as they rowed, plaintive, chanting prayers that echoed out over the dark water—*"Oh, good Mother of God, look down on us. Let there be fish!" "Oh, sweet Blessed Virgin, Mother of our God, remember us this night!"*

Suddenly, one of the men pointed out into the darkness shouting, *"Fish! Fish! Thank you, Mother of God. There are fish!"*

A companion in our boat shrugged. "He sees nothing," he said sadly. "That is just one of our customs, to bring luck. But he sees nothing. He sees no fish." Between prayers, the men muttered maledictions against the Moors, one-time captors of much of Spain, invaders who were chased from these southern shores almost five hundred years ago.

In each boat, oil-soaked flares of wood were lit and waved low over the water to attract fish. Then the flares were doused and a net dropped into the water, a single, long net with one end attached to each boat. The crew began the weary pull toward the beach, the net dragging out behind in a long, loose half-circle deep in the water. By now, the sunrise had just begun to pink the sky.

When the boats were beached, the crews worked in rhythmic teams, dragging the heavy net in from the sea. It was backbreaking work and their bare feet dug deep into the sand as they pulled. Now and then, one of the crew would life his head to shout out *"Arriba va!"* ("Up it goes!") and his trailing voice echoed over the lonely beach. Little by little, the village of Carahuela began to wake for the day. Thin smoke poured out of kitchen chimneys, a baby cried, tethered pigs grunted and rooted around a cactus hedge and little boys, barefoot and rugged, came down to the water's edge to watch the men at work.

And then the sun came out, warming away the mists from the sea and drying the clothes on the backs of the Spaniards as they tugged and pulled. The sand glistened, the Mediterranean was a crashing, brilliant blue and off to one side, in the far distance, one could see the snow-capped purple mountains outside Granada. The village itself was picturesque in the sunshine but daylight also showed the refuse-littered streets, the thin, hungry children and the harsh poverty of the homes.

By eight o'clock, the last curve of the net was near shore, but the faces of the fishermen were pinched with disappointment. The net was pulling light. The catch was small. At last, the tar-blackened meshes were dragged onto the beach with a glitter of fish in the coils. The total morning catch would barely fill a bucket. Fishermen stood silent, staring down in despair at the scanty, wriggling catch. One man crossed himself. Another muttered, "*Mother of God, have mercy on us.*"

The leader of each crew helped to divide the fish. Not enough to take to market, not enough to sell—just a double handful for each man to take to his own cottage in return for a long, chill night of hard work. The little boys on the beach were as glum as the fishermen. For a houseful of hungry children, just these few fish? Who in Carahuela would really eat that day? No fish to eat and no fish to sell; therefore no bread, no olive oil, no milk. And what would happen to the village if the Virgin could not hear the prayers tomorrow and tomorrow? There was only the sea and no other work to be had.

<<<<<<<<< >>>>>>>>>

And *this* afternoon, too, is a picture of Spain. Juan Manoja was giving a great *fiesta* for his name's day. Not on his birthday but—as is Spanish custom—on the feast day of the saint for whom he was named. He was a man of sixty, a stocky, burly farmer with a *finca* about eight miles from the nearest village. It was July and his fields stretched out, yellow and dry, in all directions from the house, with little rolling hillsides dotted with groves of silvery, twisted olive trees. The house itself sat on a low hill, three stories of whitewashed stone, fronted by a rough flagstone terrace and with windows laced over with iron grillwork and little balconies.

Juan Manoja was a prosperous, hard-working farmer who lived in the heart of his fields and close to the land.

Behind the big house were the outbuildings of the farm and a circle of simple workers' cottages ringing a manure-strewn courtyard as primitive as something out of the Middle Ages. Here donkeys brayed, children scrambled, hens pecked and housewives threw out dishwater and tablescraps in a noisy conglomeration of life. The excitement of *fiesta* was in the air. Only the male farm hands had been asked up to the big house for a glass of wine in honor of Señor Manoja, but the women honored the feast day by pinning geraniums or sprigs of jasmine in their hair.

The big house itself was clean, dark and cool, with brick floors, a few cane-seated chairs and some heavy tables and chests of dark, carved wood. In every room, large, solemn portraits of saints glowed down from the walls. Guests for the *fiesta* came from the village in old taxis or straggled over the roads on foot or *burro* (donkey) from nearby farms. It was just after high noon, hot and brilliant, and the party began with straw-covered *carafes* of local wine and squares of bread, cheese and sausage, tabled out on the great stone porch. Children hung about their parents' knees or played with cats that sauntered in from the barnyard. The mood was restful but expansive. A neighbor had brought a guitar and sat strumming in a patch of shade. Sun glinted off bright geraniums and well-filled glasses. Later in the afternoon, the whole party was served steaming rice and chicken, yellow with saffron, from earthenware tubs; then figs, green grapes and melons grown on the farm.

Juan himself was the center of the *fiesta,* passing from guest to guest with grave courtesy, his face flushed with hospitality. The noise of children, the clip-clop of donkeys' hoofs and the bleat of goats and young calves tethered near the barns made a lulling country background to the laughter and music of the party.

After lunch, the guitarist played *flamenco* music for dancing. A half dozen men sang the tunes and clapped out the stomping gypsy rhythms. Every guest danced and often the old farm hands outstayed the young men from the village, twirling and pounding. An old woman servant of the Manoja farm, her face brown and wrinkled around a toothless mouth, did a solo dance, clicking the castanets high above her head and singing out in a thin voice like a human cricket.

Much later, as the sun went down and sent cool, slanting shadows across the farmyard, the party guests and everyone from the workers' cottages crowded around the "bull ring." This was simply a big circular portion of the barnyard, walled off in white stone and used on workdays for rounding up the stock. On *fiesta* days, it is also the magic circle; a place to fight the bulls, a *corrida* in miniature.

A yearling bull, much smaller than any animal used in a true bullfight, was brought from the barn, tugging against its lead rope. When released, the bull charged about the ring, rushing at local youths who used shirts and jackets to "cape" the animal. The boys struggled to keep their courage and practice the classic bull ring passes as the bull charged past. The animal's short horns could do no serious damage but a butt from the sturdy beast would be as forceful as a brush from a small sports car. Guests clapped and roared with laughter as boy after boy went sprawling on the dry earth. The most genuine applause was saved for the *caballero* or two who stood his ground and guided the bull past him with a passably graceful flick of the "cape." It is said that every boy in Spain dreams of becoming a bullfighter, but it is often in these dusty little country rings that the close, hot breath of the bull can change a *matador's* mind.

The coolness of the early evening brought out more bread, more cheese, more wine and more music. Juan Manoja soon sat on the terrace nodding, exhausted by his own generosity. One by one, guests came to say good-by, many to walk home, five miles or more, through the dusty back roads. But the young farm hands stayed on to dance until the terrace was dark. The whole evening smelled of wine, cigarette smoke and the damp, earthy odor of geraniums. In the hot fields tomorrow and in the dusty summer days that lay ahead, this afternoon would be remembered like a cool drink of water. Juan Manoja had given his friends a great *fiesta* in the name of San Juan.

«««««« »»»»»»

And *this* also is a glimpse of Spain today: it is an ordinary Sunday afternoon and, as always, the Ramos's house on one of the side streets of Malaga is humming with life and noise. All nine children are at home today. The older girls, looking pretty and fresh in black lace head veils and pastel frocks, have just returned from High Mass at the great, brown Cathedral.

The house itself is an old one, three stories high and of white stone. Big and roomy, it is shabbily elegant, with heavy chandeliers, carved cabinets and old plush furniture, long worn smooth. The main living room is stiff and cold; the smaller family living room is crowded and comfortable, littered with books and magazines. A little radio plays classical music.

The Ramos family is a big one, a grandmother and two little maids living in the house besides the parents and nine children. At each meal, the long dining-room table is set with places for twelve. Mr. Ramos, a handsome, mustached man in his late forties, sells insurance and real estate. To help with the family budget, his wife, an astute business woman who has lived in Malaga all her life, ferrets out and sells a few antiques. Since the cost of living has gone up in Spain, it is hard to find enough money to feed and clothe a family of twelve. Every *peseta* must be watched and stretched.

Yet the atmosphere has a warm, Sunday calm. Mr. Ramos sips strong sherry from a glass the size of a small thimble as he leafs through a sports magazine. His wife, white-haired but softly pretty, embroiders at a balcony window, overlooking the broad, palm-lined street. Later in the afternoon, two of the older boys are going to watch a local soccer game, one of the older girls has a date for tennis, and the others will while away the sunny hours, working over their lessons. This is a serious, middle-class family, and all the children know they must work hard at school to learn to make a living in present-day Spain. One daughter is already a secretary in a law office and another is a clerk in a chic handbag-and-glove shop. But both finished the equivalent of our Junior College in a nearby convent school before looking for work.

In the dining room, a maid puts a low bowl of fresh carnations in the center of the table and pours water into clouded old goblets. In the kitchen, Sunday lunch is almost ready—big potato omelettes, then a thick fish soup, salad and fruit. Even on Sundays, meat is a rarity for so big a family. But the food doesn't matter. This is a happy home; busy, affectionate and untroubled. A cat plays on the balcony, a fresh bottle of sherry sits on the table, and sun winks on the tile floor.

Yet life in this house was not always so peaceful.

During the Spanish Civil War, when Señora Ramos was just a bride, she huddled grief-stricken on the same balcony while her father and brother were led from the house and shot to death in the street below. Then for four tense, horrible months, she concealed her husband in the cellar, in a tiny room with a mocked-up brick front. Just after the end of the war, their first child was born. Years of struggle followed as the battered country tried to heal the scars of civil war, years of half-poverty, half-hunger and half-fear. On this sunny Sunday afternoon of today, the Ramos' boys are excited about the soccer game, grandmother steps to the kitchen to supervise lunch, and the girls are concerned about the new school day tomorrow. Their parents rarely talk about the war.

<<<<<<<<< >>>>>>>>>

And finally *this* picture, too—and this special evening—is a part of Spain: we were guests of the Ramon Callejas, in the ancient east-coast city of Valencia. The Callejas are an old, aristocratic family, wealthy for generations from farmlands and from the acres of golden orange groves outside the town. In the summer, they escape the heat by going to their seaside villa at northern San Sebastian, near the French Border. But this was early spring and the family was at its villa in Valencia.

Spaniards are famous for their generosity, but the Callejas added a princely quality to their hospitality. The great house was set behind a high ironwork fence, in a spacious garden fragrant with flowers and towered over by palms. The marble floors of the halls and the gravel walks of the garden sounded at all hours with the faint shuffle of feet, the movement of endless little uniformed maids and housemen, busy making life pleasant and leisurely for the wealthy Callejas. Breakfast was set on the terrace with a glisten of silver; at siesta time, the fresh beds were turned down in the coolness of darkened rooms.

Señor Callejas was a busy man, working hard at "managing" rather than making money. The rest of the family did not work hard at anything; they simply went through the pampered, casual gestures of forming an appropriate background, the portrait of a wealthy, traditional family group.

Señora Callejas, exquisitely groomed, gentle and gracious, spent most of her time at home reading, embroidering, having tea with old friends and playing bridge. The only boy, Sabado, was about twenty-two, handsome and charming. He went occasionally to his father's business offices but most of the time he amused himself enjoying cars, sports and the cafe and beach life. Sabado was educated in England until he was eighteen and he had friends in London, friends in Paris, friends in Madrid. Once or twice a year, he motored down to Jerez, to join a group of wealthy friends who indulged in horse-raising and riding. Maria, the oldest daughter, was in a convent school in the south of France at the time of our visit and Pilar, a pretty, dark-haired girl of eighteen, attended a convent school in Valencia. Both lived lives as protected and watched over as are rare hothouse orchids.

When Maria went by train into France, she was accompanied by an old *dueña*, the nursemaid who had cared for the girls since childhood, and the same *dueña* went to France to bring her charge back home after each school term. Pilar lived at home and was chauffeured to and from classes each day. Neither girl was allowed to date nor to appear in public places such as the theater or main streets of the town without her parents or her brother—or the inevitable black-garbed *dueña*. Both could speak English and French as well as Spanish, both played tennis, swam and were excellent dancers. Yet neither had ever done any work more difficult than embroidering a handkerchief and neither expected to. In the Spanish tradition, these girls were being sheltered until the day their father should turn them over, protected and pampered, to a wealthy husband and a life much like the one their mother was living now.

One single evening seems to capsule Pilar's protected existence. We had all been invited to a supper dance in a Valencia hotel, in honor of the birthday of a teen-aged girl friend. Promptly at ten-thirty, the Callejas chauffeur-driven limousine pulled up before the main door of the house. Until nearly half-past eleven, we sipped sherry on a top balcony of the hotel, looking out over the twinkling lights of Valencia. In the adjoining dining room, the floor was ringed with tables and a little dance band played old American dance tunes such as *Stardust, Tea for Two* and *Nola*. It was not until the stroke of midnight that we seated ourselves at the Callejas' table and white-gloved waiters began to serve supper, a superlative banquet, punctuated with white wine, red wine and then a series of bottles of champagne. Pilar was allowed one glass of champagne, which she sipped occasionally over the hours.

At the suppertables, all the guests were seated as families. Occasionally, a male cousin sat in as an added guest but only couples formally engaged were allowed to sit together and, in that case, the young man always joined his fiancée's family. During the evening, Pilar danced with her father, her brother, a cousin—and then her father again. Though she nodded and smiled at several young men acquaintances, she spent most of the evening seated quietly between her parents at their table.

The atmosphere of the whole evening was intensely proper. The women were heavily made up and lavishly dressed in evening gowns of silk and net. Both the music and the champagne tinkled on until four in the morning but the gaiety was quiet and controlled. It was an evening of both lavishness and restraint, full of self-conscious "upper class" manners.

At four o'clock in the morning, we found the chauffeur waiting to drive us home. At the Callejas' house, lights were bright along the curved drive and in the main hall. Upstairs, a little maid in perfect uniform stood waiting to take any last-minute orders before the family retired for the night. Beside our beds stood a little table with fresh, iced fruit and cold lemonade. At the far back of the house, in the great white-tiled kitchen, a cook was lighting the first charcoal fires in the iron stove. For part of the house, a day was ending. For others, a new day had already begun.

«««««« »»»»»»»

Each of these segments is accurate, each is a glimpse of everyday life in Spain, a country of contrasts. And yet the whole picture is distinctively and proudly Spanish.

Chapter II

A COOK'S TOUR

It is possible to learn much about a country from what its people eat. A weekday menu for a working man can show something not only of the tastes of the nation but of the incomes and the products of a land.

In all of Spain, three home-grown food products stand out: olive oil, wine and oranges. The sun, the rain and the soil of Spain are right for all three crops. Olive trees line the more level fields in orderly rows, small and neat, their leaves a silvery gray-green, or they climb like mountain goats, taking root in the most unlikely patch of soil on a rocky ledge. In spite of their hardy willingness to root, these trees need careful cultivation and the tiny green spots of foliage on high mountain terraces are usually livened by the blue of a workman's shirt, as he trims branches or hoes the earth. The dead wood of olive trees is also a favorite fireplace fuel, especially in the south. In these tree-barren areas, every bit of wood is salvaged and sold at a high price. The twisted, hard wood gives little heat but it burns a long time and offers the psychological warmth of flame and sputter in a chill room.

Olive oil is the "cooking fat" of all Spain. It is used for everything from a soup base to frying fritters and many sturdy peasants are pleased to start the day with a saucer of olive oil and a piece of bread for dipping. The best grade of oil comes from the first pressing of the green olives and the pressing continues, producing lower and lower (and cheaper, of course) grades of oil until the very pits themselves are squeezed dry. Most maids or housewives buy olive oil by the day, taking an empty wine bottle to market, to be filled and brought home stoppered with a twist of paper. This interchanging of bottles brings curious results. Often the cheaper Spanish brandy tastes of olive oil and frequently the olive oil has a fine tinge of old brandy.

The higher grades of oil are smooth and excellent, while the cheaper grades are strong, have a high odor and are often very hard on the stomach. But the smell of hot olive oil is one of the most distinctive odors in all Spain.

For instance, imagine the little hill village of Benalmadena, a cluster of fifty rough white houses clinging to a hillside around a single, steepled church. At seven o'clock in the morning, the *churro lady* is outside her house, heating a deep, crusted pot of olive oil over a charcoal brazier. When the olive oil is hot enough to sputter, sending off a blue smoke and a thin, rancid odor, she drops in streams of batter that sizzle into doughnutlike fritters called *churros*. Two *churros,* strung on a piece of grass for carrying, cost about a penny. Early farm workers, riding their donkeys to the fields, may stop to buy *churros* for breakfast; little children dart out of houses with a few *pesetas* to bring home breakfast for the family. Firewood, charcoal and oil are expensive, therefore it is often cheaper to buy a bit to eat from the *churro lady* than to light a fire in the family stove.

One amusing memory about this type of breakfast: in a particular Spanish village, I noticed a well-trained dog who trotted out to the *churro* stand every morning to bring home his master's breakfast. The dog held the grass-strand carefully in his teeth and trotted off up the hill with a half-dozen *churros* dangling just above the ground. He was as meticulous as a well-trained collie bringing in the morning mail. The dog must have had a well-established charge account, since I never saw money change hands.

In Benalmadena, as is the case in most small villages, the olive oil in the *churro* pot is rarely changed, just added to as it boils away. So this village, like most others, wakes to a morning air saturated with olive oil. In varying degrees, it is the same all over Spain. Every kitchen, every back street, every country cottage lingers with the smell. And for many Spanish children, the greatest between-meals treat is a piece of hard-crusted bread, scooped almost hollow and filled with a few teaspoonfuls of olive oil.

‹‹‹‹‹‹‹‹‹ ›››››››››

The best wine in Spain once came from the sunny slopes around Malaga, but a plant disease destroyed most of the grape vines nearly one hundred years ago and now the city of Jerez de la Frontera, also in the south, is the wine and sherry center of Spain. In fact, all *true* sherry—which must meet certain high standards—comes from this area and takes its name from the corruption of the Spanish word *jerez*. Many of the brand names of Spanish wines and brandies are world-famous—TIO PEPE, FUNDADOR, VALDEPENAS AND RIOJA. Besides the bottled brands, much good local wine is sold cheaply by the *carafe* and right out of the barrel and most Spaniards like wine with their meals. Here, as in France, wine is an ordinary, casual part of the family diet. However, unlike the French, the Spaniards rarely give their children a glass, nor do Spanish women drink wine as freely as do their over-the-border French sisters. But wine and sherry, in small cafes, can be had for as little as two cents the glass.

<<<<<<<<< >>>>>>>>>

Except in the northern areas, the Spanish landscape is dotted only with olive trees—and the *other* trees, the glossy-leaved, fragrant orange trees that bring Spain one of its largest exportable crops. *Some* oranges are grown in all parts of Spain, but the major groves are around Valencia, in the east, and then through the southern fields. In the springtime, the heady fragrance of the waxy white blossoms floats in the hot air. In summer, the trees are laden with a rich crop that truly looks like balls of gold. Yet for all their "orange wealth," Spaniards do not seem to eat as many oranges as we do. Much of the crop is saved for export. I remember reading innumerable ads in newspapers in the British Isles: "Our Spanish oranges are now in! Make your marmalade now!" Yet in Spain itself, even orange juice is rarely made—except for tourists or as refreshment in cafes—and an orange is served only as dessert, along with a plum, apple or banana. The bigger, more perfect oranges—often as large as the ball used in indoor baseball—find their ways to elegant hotels and restaurants, where a skilled waiter will skin the orange quickly in one, unbroken peel, slice it thin and serve with a dust of powdered sugar. To most Americans, an orange means *juice;* in Spain, it means an exportable crop to be shipped off to orange-hungry countries not so blessed with sunlight.

※※※※※※※※ ※※※※※※※※

One could search through Spain from the northern border right down to the Mediterranean beaches and not find a single supermarket such as has become the shopping pattern in the United States.

There *are* some stores which sell varieties of things but most shops "specialize." Bread is bought at a *panadería,* milk and cheese are bought at a *lechería* and so on. The food shopper picks up one item here, another there—dropping them into a big straw shopping basket—until the day's needs are supplied. But most of the fresh things—meat, fish, fruit and vegetables—come from the main market places. There is little refrigeration (except in big homes, stores and hotels), therefore shopping is done on a "buy today, eat today" basis. Thus, daily trips to the market are somewhat social affairs, a chance to meet neighbors, exchange gossip and pick up the news of the town.

A village market is just a big-city market on a country-cousin scale. The pattern everywhere in Spain is basically the same. In a good-sized town, the market place is usually a large, roofed-over building, lined with marble-countered booths, set side by side in a labyrinth of narrow cement aisles. During shopping hours, the market is a buzz of noise and activity. At one time, it was a custom to "sing out" praise of the products and these singing commercials added to the din, but now this practice is banned by law. Such laws, however, have not prevented the food sellers from calling out encouragement to any shopper who pauses to examine a bunch of carrots or thump a melon. Stalls are grouped together according to the type of produce sold, so that one may look down the special aisles arranged with dozens and dozens of eggs, bushels of apples and symmetrical pyramids of cabbages. The color, smell and beauty of the masses of products is always exciting.

What can one find to buy in a good-sized market? In the fish stalls, heaps of clams, pink shrimp and big, pink-shelled crayfish, also long, gray-tentacled squid, silvery sardines and tiny whitebait, which are fried and eaten head and all, and striped tuna so big that it must be sliced like beef. Then there are big, white-fleshed merluzza or hake, and codling, a small but fierce-looking fish which is prepared by clamping its jaws onto its tail and frying in a "vicious circle"—and dozens of other silvered, slithering "fruits of the sea." The fish are sold *al fresco,* or "natural," heads, tails, scales and all, wrapped in a bit of newspaper and cleaned in the family kitchen. The only prepared fish sold in the market are the giant flaps of cod, opened out, flatted and dried and salted, then stacked in heaps like old chamois skins. Salt cod is a blessing to the poor man's budget. Even though there is not much fish taste left, it is salty and filling to the stomach. It makes a good base for a fish soup and, steam-cooked in a sauce of tomatoes, garlic and peppers, it becomes a delectable dish.

Because of the lack of refrigeration, meat is usually sold shortly after butchering and the meat stalls are hung with almost undistinguishable half-carcasses of beef, lamb, pork or goat. Most Spaniards prefer small cuts of meat—individual chops, fillets or cutlets—rather than roasts—and many bits and pieces are sold simply to flavor a rice or vegetable dish. Meat, on the daily budget, is a very expensive item.

In special festoons, hung by their hind legs, are skinned young kid and rabbit. In smaller markets, the furred paws are usually left on the rabbits, to prove to the customer that this is *not* strayed cat. I was always especially amused by the great, fat, well-scrubbed pigs' heads for sale, although I never learned how they were cooked. But the pig, in the repose of its butcher-block death, has a silly, grinning look, as if the animal is self-conscious about being caught in this position in the first place.

Poultry is routine, although often scrawny: ducks, chickens and a few turkeys, with wild pheasant and partridge in season. Occasionally, a number of hens or a noisy rooster are tethered right in the poultry stall, very vocal and very much alive. It is the refrigeration problem again. A live bird is much more fresh than an unsold bird strung up by his legs, waiting for a customer—who may not come until tomorrow.

The fruit section always has the aroma and color of a florist shop, for the Spanish sun is kind to fruits. Lemons, oranges, bananas, apples, peaches, pears, cherries, strawberries and grapes are plentiful, and even more common to the Spanish table—because they grow in the home garden, right among the flowers—are figs and pomegranates. In the middle of the summer, melons are magnificent, and the Spanish watermelon is even better than ours. It is much smaller and rounder and very sweet but fresh. Later in the summer, the bright pink pear of the prickly cactus comes into the market. Many are gathered wild along the country roadsides. These pears are so sweet that they almost bring tears to the eyes and they are usually rinsed down with a quick drink of cold water.

Vegetables run the gamut from potatoes to tomatoes, including almost everything known to the American kitchen except corn-on-the-cob. Artichokes are common and superb. They are not often given the upper-class treatment of boiling, chilling

A Cook's Tour - 23

and serving with a delicate Hollandaise sauce. More often, they are cut up for soups, stews and cold salads or cooked as a second vegetable, to be served with meat. Eggplant, in the right season, almost ousts the white potato on the menus, and Spaniards like little green peppers, fried whole in oil and garlic and eaten seeds and all. Garlic is a cooking essential here, used heavily in village kitchens and with more subtlety by those who find its after-odor antisocial.

Food there is, in variety and in plenty, but unfortunately—for many Spaniards—there is frequently more food than spending money.

«««««« »»»»»»»

In Spain, the living hours—and hence the dining hours—are so different from ours that Spaniards might almost be using a different clock. In the simplest villages and farms, where electricity is expensive or there is none at all, life is lived with the sun. In most other places, the day begins with breakfast at nine or ten o'clock and continues until midnight, one o'clock or long after. I remember waking one morning at about two in a balconied hotel room on the Rambla, in Barcelona. The broad street below seemed so noisy that I thought there might have been an accident. Not at all. It was simply the social noises of the evening. Crowds were still sitting in cafes, wandering slowly through the warm summer night or chatting under the trees on folding wooden chairs, rented for a *peseta* or two. In Barcelona, it was just too early for bed.

Breakfast in Spain is always light; usually *cafe con*

leche—half-hot coffee, half-hot milk and lots of sugar, plus bread and butter with marmalade or honey. Ham and eggs, fruit juices and most cereals are simply not considered as breakfast foods. And I never saw a pancake or waffle in all Spain.

After breakfast, the workday begins, broken for a late luncheon at two or even three o'clock in the afternoon. Many travelers are weak with hunger by the time the Spanish lunch hour arrives, but most Spaniards can get through that part of the day without so much as a coffee break. In Madrid, Barcelona and other big cities, American-type snack bars have become popular; but in hotels or in smaller towns, an approach to a restaurant or hotel dining room before one o'clock will bring looks of pained surprise from the waiters. At that hour, the little maids are still in the back courtyard, ironing the damp table linen, and the cook in the kitchen is still chopping the garlic.

Luncheon, when it is finally served, is the major meal of the day and it is a generous one. Few Spaniards are diet-conscious; in fact, a plump woman is invariably considered *más guapa* ("more pretty") than a slim one. So Spanish luncheons are meant to be lingered over and enjoyed, from first to fifth course.

As an example (and, of course, the possibilities are varied) of luncheon served in some cool, dark-paneled dining room or on an airy terrace patterned with shadows, one might begin with *entremeses.* This is an array of tidbits, each served on a separate plate, which could include sliced red sausage, cold shrimps in the shell, potatoes with mayonnaise, sliced tomatoes, salted almonds, green olives, tiny hot meat balls, sliced dry ham, cucumbers, little clams and sliced hard-boiled eggs. Next, an egg or fish course. The eggs might be baked in open ramekins with a bit of ham, some peas, pimiento and tomatoe sauce, or they might be blended in a delicate gold omelette folded around ham, mushrooms or cheese. The fish could be cold *merluzza*, served with mayonnaise and capers, or *pescados variados* ("mixed fish")—a platter of fried *merluzza*, bream, sardines and tiny fish called *chanquetes*, fried whole and looking like a heap of crumbled cornflakes.

The meat course is probably a chop or a slice of beef or veal, fried like a small steak, with green peas, carrots and halved artichokes; then a lettuce and tomato salad, simple and fresh.

Dessert most commonly begins with a large mixed bowl of fresh fruit, from which each diner will select an orange or a banana and perhaps a few grapes and ripe figs. In many homes and in most small restaurants, fruit is served unwashed, with a large bowl of fresh water on the table for dipping. This is both to cool the fruit and make it *muy fresco,* "very fresh," and to rinse it, but I always found it disconcerting to dip a bunch of grapes in the bowl and wash off an ant or two or perhaps a dormant wasp which revived with the water. Cheese follows fruit and it may be one of many types, possibly orange *bolla* or *manchega,* the latter a sturdy, hard cheese made of goat's milk. And finally, cakes and tarts, which are usually turned down with a satisfied *no, gratias!* and sent back to the kitchen to save for tea.

Dinner in the evening, as one might expect, is light—soups, salads or eggs and fruit—and it is rarely served before nine or ten o'clock. Even little children often toddle around until this late dinner hour. In homes with large staffs, eleven o'clock is decidedly the more fashionable time. Elaborate Spanish homes often have two sets of kitchen help— one group serving from breakfast through luncheon, the other group on duty for tea through dinner. With such heavy dining, it might be well to have a double shift of diners, too!

«««««« »»»»»»

These long Spanish hours are made pleasant and yawn-free by two things typically Spanish—the afternoon *siesta* and the cafes.

The *siesta*, of course, is an afternoon nap. By law, all businesses must be closed for a minimum of two hours during the working day and most shops shutter their doors from one until three o'clock. This leaves time for dining *and* resting. In the summertime, when the heat is high, a *siesta* behind cool, closed shutters is almost the only way to get through a hot day. In the winter, a warm bed is a welcome midafternoon retreat in a chilly, marble-floored apartment or a wind-beaten hillside cottage. Around construction jobs or far off in the countryside, *siesta* time is often observed on the spot, with workers curling up on a heap of cement sacks or finding the shade of an olive tree to enjoy the free time alloted them by custom and by law.

In the cities—and in prosperous villages—the post-*siesta* hours, when the streets begin again to swarm with people, always prove a refreshing time. Rested faces, fresh lipstick, clean shirts and the sweet, flowery scent of Spanish cologne brighten the whole afternoon. With the midday rest, the Spanish day really begins twice—and the second half is marked for family life and pleasure. However, not every Spaniard can take time to sleep. A farmer delivering vegetables by donkey to some mountain town may plod on through the gray winter rain or an overworked housewife may need the *siesta* hours simply to keep her family clean and fed. But the *siesta* is a custom observed whenever possible.

The Spanish cafe is another institution which keeps life geared to a leisurely pace. These cafes are not quite like our bars or taverns; they are more like clubs, social spots away from home where a man may relax, discuss business and find himself among friends. In larger cities, cafes may be modern, impersonal and jammed until two or three in the morning; in a country village, the single cafe may be no more than a half dozen rickety tables and chairs set under a canopy of sugar cane. But the companionship is always there. Except in larger cities, cafes are exclusively "men's clubs," with never a female inside the doors. But in the big cities, more free and more sophisticated, the cafe is the logical termination for women after a leisurely stroll through the parks or crowded streets. A woman is always accompanied by the man in her life, of course. In Madrid, for instance, the cafes along the Gran Via are filled every Sunday night with elegantly groomed men and women who have been out for a long social walk. To finish the evening, they stop to enjoy drinks or coffee and to look or be looked at.

In the morning, the businessman may pause for a cup of strong, sweet coffee while he looks over the morning papers; a workman may find his favorite cafe for a glass of white wine or a shot of strong, warming anis before starting on the job. And in the evening, in the long pre-dinner hours, a man feels very lucky sitting over an aperitif or *vino,* talking, smoking and eating a bite of *tapis.*

A Spaniard is as relaxed in his favorite cafe as in his own home. When houses are small or apartments crowded with children, the cafe serves as an extra room, an addition to several hundred homes at once. It also offers a man that sip and snack that can satisfy his hunger until the late dinner hour.

At most cafes, in the late afternoon until closing, a bit of special food is presented with each drink. These *tapis* consist of a variety of appetizing tidbits such as a sliver of steak in sauce, olives or almonds, a cold salted shrimp, a slice of sausage, fried squid and even tiny roasted sparrows. In a certain section of Madrid, every street is lined with open-fronted cafes specializing in different *tapis* and until early morning, the streets flow with people, sipping a glass of wine with steak here, a glass of wine with sardines there. The cafe custom does not necessarily mean heavy drinking, however, and one glass may well last an evening. The cafe custom means that a man's home is as big as his own town—with his favorite cafe added as the front window.

〈〈〈〈〈〈〈〈〈   〉〉〉〉〉〉〉〉〉

Spanish food, unlike Mexican food, is not usually highly spiced or hotly seasoned. Much of the cooking is done on wood or charcoal fires, often small ones, so a kind of "stewing" cooking predominates in many homes. In the northern areas, where there are better grazing lands, the meat is good but in the south, it is of a lesser quality and quite expensive. Luckily, however, with its miles of coast line, Spain is never without a good supply of fresh, varied fish.

Here are just a few of the country's specialties: in the Basque north, huge crabs called *centollas* are favorites. The meat is removed, chopped up and replaced for cooking and then served with a spiced sauce. *Calamares en su tinta* are tiny squid, cut up in bits and cooked in their own "ink," that curious black liquid emitted by squid. This dish is delicious and full of flavor but it is the only food I can think of, except caviar, that is a dark, final black in color. *Angulas* is another fish specialty and the sign *Hay angulas!* ("Here are *angulas!*") is enough to start a rush on any restaurant. *Angulas* are tiny eel spawn, silvery and so minute that about a dozen could fit easily in a teaspoon. *Angulas* are cooked in an earthen dish, with olive oil and a few slivers of garlic and hot red peppers, to be eaten sizzling hot with a wooden fork.

Soup is always good in Spain and from the standpoint of the non-Spanish chef the soup base is interesting; almost every pot of soup begins with a few teaspoonfuls of olive oil. This makes the soup nourishing and "meaty" even when little meat is used. Both *my* favorite soups are cold *sopa de ajo* or "garlic soup," made of finely pounded garlic, white almonds, bread crumbs, oil and vinegar, and *gazpacho*, a soup with an oil, vinegar and bread-crumb base to which finely chopped tomatoes, green peppers and onions are added. Both are peasant soups, served in farmhouses across Spain, but both also appear in the best restaurants, usually with the soup bowl resting in a second bowl of cracked ice for complete chilling.

A *cocida* (the word means simply "cooked") is usually a delicious big dish of *garbanzo*, or chick peas, cooked in a casserole with onions and tomato sauce and accompanied by both black and red sausages, ham, beef, a bit of salt pork, cabbage, carrots, leeks and other ingredients, all of which have been cooked together. The rich soup of this melange is usually served first at a meal, with black bread and sliced bones with marrow to use as a bread-spread. The gigantic second course follows and it is a dish big enough to serve a large family, plus the clutter of little maids in the kitchen necessary to prepare it. *Paella*, which is reputedly at its best in the rice-growing country around Valencia, is certainly the national dish of Spain. *Paella* can be simple or superb, depending on how many items are added to it—but it is always filling and good. It is a rice dish, seasoned and yellowed with saffron, in which are cooked bits of pork and chicken, green peas, pimientos and artichokes, shrimps and little clams in their shells. Many Spanish families serve *paella* as their standard Sunday luncheon, prefaced by individual potato omelettes and all washed down with local white wine. No wonder the afternoon *siesta* has become a custom!

<<<<<<<<<< >>>>>>>>>>

To know *all* about what is eaten in Spain, one should look at the other side of the menu. But, unfortunately, the other side of the average "poor man's" menu often has little on it. Too many of the people of the country are forced, through lack of money, to eat simply or too lightly. Living contrasts here are great and the lavish luncheon in some homes is balanced off by the thin soup and hard bread in others. The market may be heaped with food—but a man must find work to earn *pesetas* to buy it. And, since the average laboring man's daily take-home pay is only about a dollar, many tables are set extremely lightly. Only shrewd economy and cooking skill keep many families fed at all. Of course, in most countries in the world this problem of earning enough for food is a constant one. But it seems important to make it clear that all Spaniards are not plump, food-loving folk, dining each day on hams, suckling pigs and sparklingly red wine.

I clearly remember one day when I took a short cut through some farmland, from our *villa* down to the town. Under a tree was a young mother in dust-grayed black and her small son. They had just seated themselves for lunch. She broke a large piece of crusty bread in two pieces while the boy skinned and split a stalk of fresh sugar cane he had just cut in the field. Both smiled, nodded and passed the time of day with me as I went by. They seemed very content with themselves and their picnic on that hot, still day.

Chapter III

SPANISH FIESTAS—PAGEANTRY, PINWHEELS AND PRAYERS

Spaniards love holidays or *fiestas*. There is hardly a day on the Spanish calendar that is not marked as a special saint's day and therefore hardly a day goes by without a church, town or a province —or all the Joses and Trinidads in the country— celebrating a holy day. Almost everything and everyone has a patron saint and saints' days are usually celebrated instead of individual birthdays.

Of course, "holiday" is a verbal corruption of "holy day" but the festivities are often marked more by gaiety than piety. Some Spanish holidays still *do* mean church candles and incense, but many others now mean only firecrackers, fun and flowers.

There are many reasons why holidays are so popular. Spaniards are hard workers and time off is always welcome. They enjoy good grooming, dressing up and looking attractive; a *fiesta* is a pleasant excuse to put on a clean shirt or a pastel dress and promenade in the streets. Many Spaniards are short of *pesetas* and, since a *fiesta* is usually a village or group affair, it is possible to join the activities without spending too much money. Most of all, the high spirits of the Spaniards make them perfect people for loud, bright and late-night celebrating.

Fiestas are both big and small, rocking a whole city with their noise or lighting up a few candles in an isolated mountain village. Some last a day, some last a week. In most *fiestas,* the pattern of the celebration has existed from decades to centuries, and the ritual of the festivity is the same year after year.

<<<<<<<<< >>>>>>>>>

One of the most important holidays in all Spain in *Semana Santa,* the Holy Week ceremonies preceding Easter Sunday. Every town and every village has its own religious processions but people from all over Spain crowd into the bigger towns of Seville and Malaga, to take part in their picturesque *Semana Santa.*

Malaga, a city of over a quarter of a million people, is a southern port town of the Mediterranean. It is so old that Roman ruins still stand behind the great Cathedral and Columbus passed in triumph through its streets, on his way back to Granada after his first voyage to America. Today, the city is a mixture of very old, narrow and crooked streets and some newer, wider boulevards in the business section and near the waterfront. Here *Semana Santa* is a spectacle never to be forgotten.

Preparations begin early. For several weeks ahead, special alleyways or corners of public parks are covered with great spreads of ballooning canvas, like circus tenting. Inside, crews of volunteers are at work, assembling huge floats that will be part of the processions.

Floats carry two separate sets of religious groupings: during the first days, the Blessed Virgin, with an angelic attendant or two, is paraded through the streets. On Good Friday, the floats carry only statuary scenes of the Crucifixion of Jesus Christ.

These floats are huge wooden structures, like giant stretchers made of timber, sometimes taking as many as three hundred men to carry them. Each float is sponsored by a church parish, a workers' group (the Carpenters Guild, the *Guardia Civil*, etc.) or by special religious clubs. The same props are reassembled each year, touched up with gilt paint, polished, decked with flowers and candles. And, of course, since the statue of the Virgin is dressed in real robes, the heavenly garments must be pressed, darned and refurbished.

A bare float, during assembling, may look like a bulky gold raft, waiting for its glittering cargo. Along the sides are brackets for candles and enough hidden vases for hundreds of flowers. A great wooden-spoked rack, like a peacock's tail in repose, is arranged to hold out the Virgin's train. The huge statues are brought from churches at the last hour, wired into place and given a final trim of jewels and flowers. One favorite Malaga Virgin is paraded proudly with a damaged face and shattered hands. She withstood the bombings of the Civil War and now benignly resumes her place as a protectress of the town.

The first two nights of *Semana Santa* are subdued, almost like a dress rehearsal, but by Wednesday night the city is jammed from ten o'clock until three in the morning, and every street reverberates with the roll of drums and the high, triumphant notes of trumpets. The route of the processions is lined wih folding chairs, rented by the evening, and every balcony is either rented out—sometimes at fancy prices to tourists—or crowded with Malaguenians. Besides the religious floats, the procession is made up of elegantly dressed bands, usually in medieval costumes, and followed by groups of *penitentes,* men dressed in monklike robes of white, black, green or red, tied at the waist with a cord and with a tall peaked and draped mask with slits for eyes. Each *penitente* carries a lit candle and the sight of hundreds and hundreds of hooded marchers, moving to the melancholy roll of drums, gives the procession an eerie tone of the Middle Ages.

In Malaga, there are many churches; hence many statues of the Blessed Virgin. Each is arrayed in her best garments for Holy Week. By custom, these statues of the Virgin—like earthly well-dressed women—have many changes of wardrobe, simple garments for every day and heavily embroidered, elaborate costumes for church holidays. Also the Virgins have individual *personalities* painted right on their faces —some Virgins look middle-aged and worried, others are representations of the *young* Mother of God, slim and lovely, and still other statues depict the brokenhearted, suffering Mother on Calvary, with tears streaming down Her cheeks. But for *Semana Santa,* each Virgin is dressed in her best— flowing gown, jeweled velvet cape and glittering crown. And each float, assembled with love, piety and pride—plus tradition—shines with candles and is fragrant with flowers.

«««««« »»»»»»

Spaniards often refer to Our Lord, Jesus Christ— respectfully and warmly as *El Señor,* meaning "Sir" or "Lord." On Good Friday evening all the floats carry statues of the crucified and suffering *El Señor,* draped in mournful black. There is no music this night, just the melancholy roll of drums and the clack of wood blocks, like heavy castanets, to mark the hours of procession and shuffling feet.

The great floats, carried shoulder-high, swing and rock with the motion of the human bodies beneath, often giving the statues a disturbing lifelike sway. At a distance, moving down the long streets, the brightly-lit platforms look like sorrowful boats rocking on a dark sea.

Special rituals mark this religious week: on one night a prisoner is freed from the local jail in honor of the Good Thief who died with Jesus Christ long ago. The singing of *sietas,* or songs of penance, is another custom. Except on Good Friday, the procession is often interrupted by these chants, sung out from some balcony or doorway. The songs may be sung spontaneously by someone moved with piety or a heavy conscience, but more often they are traditional songs, intoned by a pious Spaniard who also happens to have a good singing voice. The serenaded Virgin on her float always pauses to listen to these lyrical prayers, thus giving her weary bearers a chance to rest.

Semana Santa is always a serious religious festival and the atmosphere is subdued; voices are hushed, spectators are devout. Most women wear black, with veiling, and no Spanish man would stand with head covered as the Virgin or El Señor passes by.

The giant dramatic scenes of the large cities are repeated in miniature at least one night in every little village in Spain. There the Virgin from the local church is taken on a nighttime tour of the streets, followed by the whole populace, carrying candles and singing hymns. In the mountain villages, viewed from a peak or high curve in the road, these processions of pin-point light are an eerie sight. But at close view, it is always an intense and personal affair. The village Virgin is as familiar to most of the people as a member of their own families.

Perhaps this small experience will illustrate the truly intimate devotion of many Spaniards. Late one Good Friday evening I was standing on a balcony with a Spanish friend. Below us, a statue of Christ crucified was being carried past us in reverent silence. Suddenly, my friend sang out the first notes of a *sieta*, then stopped short, whispering, *"Perdón, El Señor. Yo he olvidado!"* ("Pardon me, Lord. I forgot!"). One does not sing to a suffering Christ and my friend's apology was a personal, heartfelt one.

«««««« »»»»»»»

Occasionally, Spanish planning ends with accidents that must make even El Señor smile. He may even have chuckled at this one: hundreds of villages present the Passion Play, using whatever local talent and props are available. A certain mountain village was too poor to present its own play, so an amateur theatrical group from a larger town came out to aid the villagers. Now Holy Week is traditionally a time for fasting and sober living, but the villagers went all out to show a welcome. The best house in town was turned over to the guests, plus round-the-clock offerings of coffee and food.

The dramatic group brought with them all stage props except one item they felt could be had easily in the village, i.e. a small, humble donkey. But the villagers' hearts were bursting with generosity. No *little donkey* was good enough for Holy Week and El Señor. Right on cue, they pushed onto the stage, not a donkey, but the town's biggest, sleekest, healthiest mule. The oversized beast lacked both humility and acting ability. Its entrance knocked over the pillars of Pontius Pilate's court—and from then on it sat stubbornly midstage through the entire play, refusing to budge even for El Señor.

❮❮❮❮❮❮❮❮❮ ❯❯❯❯❯❯❯❯❯

In Valencia, the *Fallas of San José*—held during the week in March in which Saint Joseph's name day falls—are as hectic and exuberant as *Semana Santa* is sobering and subdued. The town goes wild. During the week, most businesses and offices are closed after lunch and, in the main streets and squares, no motor traffic is allowed.

The *fallas* (the word means "bonfire" really) are competitive groups of statues, huge things made of cardboard, wax and bright paints, to be carried in parade . . . much like the figures promenaded in the Macy's Parade on Thanksgiving Day in New York City. The Valencian groups often lampoon current political figures, movie stars, tourists, Valencians—anything for a satirical laugh. During the week, the giant images are paraded through the streets to the accompaniment of music, firecrackers and general noise.

All the most beautiful girls in Valencia are candidates for various queenships: Queen of Music, Queen of Flowers or Queen of Arts, and great balls are held with the queens presiding. It is a gay time of silk dresses, lacy mantillas and fresh flowers.

On the last night of the *fiesta*, all the *fallas* are set aflame—about one hundred and fifty of them—dimming even the brightest electric lights of the town and turning the night sky pink. The celebration of the *Fallas of San José* is much like our Mardi Gras, raucous, carefree and colorful. It is an extremely extrovert *fiesta*. I feel that Saint Joseph might easily be too shy and unworldly to attend his feast in person.

<<<<<<<<< >>>>>>>>>

From the standpoint of beauty alone, Spain's top *fiesta* is the *feria* of Seville (the fair), held every spring. This is a week-long celebration—held shortly after Easter—that fills the whole city with crowds, flowers, gypsies, horses, bullfights and beautiful *señoritas*. The southern city of Seville itself has often been called "the beautiful woman of Spain." It is an ancient town of white, graceful buildings, laced with iron balconies and window grills, the whole split through the middle by the River Guadilquiver. The mammoth gray cathedral is the most spectacular in all Spain and it is here that Christopher Columbus is entombed. Every day, 500 Masses are said in the eighty chapels and the streets around the structure are lined with tiny cafes, so people may rest, sip wine and admire this giant work of art. Seville is a hot town, splendid with flowers, so that even the springtime nights of the *fiesta* are warm and scented.

During the *feria*, distinguished families from all over Spain set up large, housekeeping tents in the vacant lots and side streets of the town, "at home" to greet friends, serve refreshments and dance Andalusian dances far into the night. Men wear the traditional Andalusian costume of tight black trousers, red waist band, white shirt with short black jacket and Cordoban hat. The women are costumed as glamorous gypsies, in long ruffled dresses, high combs and mantillas. Even though the *feria* here attracts thousands of tourists, it is not an attraction mocked-up only for travelers. It is Spanish through and through. A tourist may join the cafe crowds, go to bullfights and wander through the gay streets, to peek into tents alive with dancers and gaiety, but the *feria* is a time for Spaniards to enjoy themselves and entertain their friends. Fortunately, Spanish hospitality is quick and many lonely tourists find themselves included as "friends."

This spring *feria* of Seville schedules a *corrida* (a program of six bullfights) every afternoon of the week, and this period launches the busy season for most *matadors*. Every bullfighter is eager to start his work year with good newspaper notices from Seville, and a fine showing there can mean choice bookings all over the country until the final *corrida* in October.

Fiestas in Spain are not just for *some* people, they are for *everyone*. They can fill a whole town, or an entire *barrio*, because most city districts or suburbs celebrate *their* special patron's holiday, too. One day late in August, we drove into a Spanish town and registered at an attractive *pension* on a side street. It was a quiet, sunny day. At four o'clock—right after *siesta* time—we walked out into the small central plaza and suddenly the air was split with the noise and smell of firecrackers. Strings of crackers had been run on wires from lamp-post to lamp-post and tree to tree, around the square and up the side streets. When the first cracker was lit, the others popped off in chain fashion, snapping in the air or whipping like snakes along the street. Within a minute, the whole section was awakened to *fiesta*. Like a gun going off, the signal for fun had begun and our adopted "neighborhood" did not know a moment's quiet for the next two days. With firecrackers over our heads and around our ankles, we were automatically drawn into the whole joyous confusion.

<<<<<<<<<< >>>>>>>>>>

Many a rural Spaniard may live and die without seeing a major *feria* in Madrid, San Sebastian or Seville—but no Spaniard could live without his annual local *fiesta*. Even the smallest village has some celebration at least once a year.

Recently, we went to the annual fair in Churriana, a small but fairly prosperous village in the country. The town square and all adjoining streets had been transformed into a midway, with strings of colored lights, and a traveling carnival had set up miniature Ferris wheels, merry-go-rounds, shooting galleries and candy stands. The fair opened with a blessing by the parish priest, a few rounds of firecrackers, and continued for five days, with the streets jammed until three every morning.

Most of the carnival rides cost two cents and the shooting galleries offered three shots for a penny, with a cigarette or piece of candy as the prize. Sidewalk refreshment stands, hung with glaring bare bulbs, sold fair-time specialties such as halved coconuts, candied fruits and squares of marzipan. Many Churrianians spent every night of the fair promenading through the glaring streets or sitting at a cafe, in whole families down to the smallest infant, sipping wine and lemonade. Every corner of the village echoed with five days of festivity.

«««««« »»»»»»»

Some town fairs are more markedly religious than others, especially if the town has a famous patron saint or a well-known Virgin. (All "Virgins" are, of course, the one Mother of Jesus Christ, represented through statues, but people of various areas are wont to give *their* Virgin special powers, personalities and attributes.)

The Virgin of Cartama, for instance, is a great favorite because she is rumored to be a good listener; people of the town and countryside round about believe this Virgin is especially attentive to prayers and favors requested. Throughout the year, men and women promise a "pilgrimage to Cartama" in return for cures for sore throats, business success, luck with the crops and so forth, blessings which they feel came to them through the intercession of the Virgin of Cartama with her Divine Son in their behalf. This particular Virgin is called "Our Lady of Remedies" and her statue is said to be over five hundred years old.

Cartama itself is a mountain village, with the Virgin's shrine set at the peak above the town. Pious pilgrims often walk miles barefoot to the shrine, climbing up the last rocky steps on their bare knees. At the opening of the *fiesta* of Cartama, the statue of the Virgin is brought into the heart of town, accompanied by the priest, a dozen altar boys and hundreds of pilgrims carrying candles.

We visited Cartama the opening night of the fair. As we neared the town, the road was spotted with pilgrims on foot and on donkeys, and every curve was crowded with chartered buses. A crown of lights around the mountaintop shrine showed first, then a wavering, winding line of candles tracing down toward town.

The town square itself was kept dark, closed in on three sides by two-story white houses. The church bell tolled vibrantly through the night and the statue of the Blessed Virgin was paraded about the square on a heavy gilt throne, carried by thirty men. Banks of candles were gusted and flattened by the wind. A thin Moorish music with a heavy drumbeat marked the rythmn of the march and the mood was somber and funereal. As the statue of the Virgin circled the square, silent crowds surged after it or stared down from balconies hung with Mary's colors, gilt and blue. At last the Virgin was placed in the lower church, to preside over the three-day fair.

Typical carnival mood and trappings filled the

rest of the village. Every cafe was crowded with families, eating late dinners of homemade bread and sausage, sipping wine right out of the straw-covered jugs. At the village dance, a three-piece orchestra beat out musical numbers popular in America twenty years ago. As the night wore on, pilgrims put on their shoes and joined the dance.

The *fiesta* was split distinctly into two parts: serious religious ceremonies for Our Lady of Remedies first, and worldly relaxation second. On the last day, to take advantage of the many travelers and farmers who had come to town, Cartama held its annual mule and donkey auction in a nearby field.

<<<<<<<< >>>>>>>>

One of the most moving *fiestas* I saw in all Spain was at a fishing village on the Mediterranean. This village was bitterly poor, a huddle of houses separated by a single street of sand and rock. Once a year, in prayerful procession, the villagers follow their statue of the Virgin down to the sea, imploring her help and protection for the coming year.

At about ten at night, the simple statue was carried from the church, preceded by the priest and altar boys in ragged vestments swinging incense lamps. The procession moved at a snail's pace through the street and out onto the beach. As the statue of the Virgin neared the water, many women began calling out to the Mother of God with earnest, personal pleas, tears running down their cheeks, hands clasped tensely around their candles. These women were *begging* the Virgin to hear them, begging for safety for their fishermen husbands and a decent living in the coming year.

It was a moonless night and the dark, crashing waves of the sea looked ominous and unfriendly as the bearers dipped the statue so the Virgin's feet were touched with spray.

Later, the rickety, cane-roofed cafe attracted a few male wine drinkers but this was a quiet *fiesta*. Not many families had more money to spare than the few *pesetas* it took to buy candles to follow the Virgin.

«««««««« »»»»»»»»

A *romeria* is a special kind of *fiesta* and a very gay one. The word means both "pilgrimage" and "picnic"—and it is both. It is, in short, a spring or summer picnic, held in some special spot in the countryside that seems particularly blessed. One *romeria,* for instance, ended around the great spring that irrigated many of the farm fields of the area; another chose a fertile olive grove as its picnic site. A *romeria* is an all-day affair, beginning right after Mass (it is always on a Sunday or holy day) and usually ending with Benediction, officiated at by the local priest, right at the picnic site.

For this day, Spanish girls dress in their most elaborate costumes; even the three-year-olds have ruffled and dotted dresses, flowers and fans. The boys are garbed as the *caballeros* at the Seville *feria*. Farm carts are draped like covered wagons, then pinned and wound with colored paper and flowers; horses and mules are bridled with fresh blossoms.

Whole groups or families make the trip in the wagons, while *novia* and *novio* (engaged couples) go on mule or horseback, the boy guiding the animal while his *novia* sits sidesaddle behind him, skirt spread out, one hand on hip and head held high in arrogant "gypsy" fashion. Those without transportation simply go on foot. The bright caravan trails up the roads to the picnic ground. There the celebrating crowd spread lunches under the trees to spend the day feasting, singing and dancing. Who goes on the *romeria?* Just everyone. Students vacationing from the universities, the boy who helps in his father's butcher shop, a local widow with her twelve children, two seamstresses from the lower village—anyone who can play the castanets, dance, laugh or just enjoy watching.

<<<<<<<<< >>>>>>>>>

The endless *fiestas* of Spain are an ancient and important part of life here. No one seems too old or too young to feel the spirit. A true Spanish *fiesta* covers an area like a bright tent. Everyone becomes part of the show.

Chapter IV

SPANISH CUSTOMS: BLACK BANDS TO BOMBAS

COUNTRIES, like people, have personalities. They show their hearts and their faces in many little ways. A country's customs, habits, whims and superstitions—those bits and pieces of everyday life—give a glimpse of what the people feel and think, what they are like "inside."

What, for instance, is more typical of Spain and the grace of Spanish people than the custom of the *piropo*?

A *piropo* is simply a compliment and, as they walk the crowded streets or kick the dust of a country road, Spanish men like to toss out graceful *piropos* like fresh spring flowers. This compliment is never bold, it is rarely personal. Rather, it is a few flattering words whispered into the breeze as men and women pass each other. The girl never acknowledges the words, except perhaps by a faint smile, but she always hears them and is, in fact, waiting for them. Would it not be a waste of beauty and good spirits if a shiny-haired *señorita* in a fresh, colorful dress, touched lightly with cologne and trimmed with a sprig of jasmine behind the ear, did not get *some* appreciation?

«««««« »»»»»»

The simple and most common type of *piropo* is just *que quapa!* or "what beauty!" but the skilled piropoist can do much better than that. At best, the compliment is spontaneous; the complimenter is moved by the beauty and charm of the admired to say whatever comes first to his lips. "You are lovelier than red roses," or "My eyes cannot believe what they see" or "Someone is lucky to know you as a friend"—just short phrases of praise, murmured in passing.

But the *piropo* has nothing to do with that American-type gesture of appreciation, the "wolf whistle." The *piropo* is subtle, quick and respectful; just between two people, not the whole street. It is never meant to embarrass and it is never meant to start an acquaintance—the man whispers his compliment and continues on his way.

And what, exactly, is likely to inspire a *piropo?* Spain has pretty girls by the thousands and well-groomed, graceful girls by the additional thousands. A pretty face or figure usually earns *piropos,* plus any little touch of femininity that attracts attention —a pair of high clicking heels, a full swinging skirt, flowers in the hair or dangling earrings. And when would a pretty girl not be offered a *piropo?* If she is with her parents or a chaperone, if she is walking with or tending children or if she is already with the young man of her choice. The best *piropo* must have a bit of mystery, a sense of challenge and romance. It will never interfere with a girl's sense of propriety or her privacy.

«««««« »»»»»»

Many *piropos* are exaggerated, flowery and touched with the poetic. A young Spanish friend of mine told me seriously of a *piropo* he overheard. It had filled him with admiration: a girl was walking down the boulevard, head erect, eyes ahead and a man passed her with this whisper, "Ah, you are more graceful than Manolete in his greatest day in the bull ring!"

"How much more flattering," said my friend, "than simply telling the *senorita* that she was another pretty girl!"

«««««« »»»»»»

The word *novia* (the male counterpart is *novio*) is an important one in Spain. It means "fiancée" and also "bride" and, since the romantic life of young Spaniards is closely watched over by custom and the rules of the Catholic Church, the acceptance of a *novia* is a big step.

Teen-aged boys and girls, in all economic groups, are rarely allowed to spend time alone together until they are firmly—and with family approval—declared *novia* and *novio*. In this country, there is almost no casual dating, going to movies, driving around in cars or staying out late.

A twenty-four-year-old girl living in Madrid, for instance, outlined her social life this way: "On holidays or weekends, groups of young people might get together to go to the beach, play tennis or go to the cinema. On Sunday afternoons, there might be a tea dance at a hotel. But I am usually home by eight o'clock, certainly not later than ten, and we go home in groups. At ten o'clock, the front door to our apartment building is locked and if I reach home later than that, I have to clap my hands for the *sereno,* or nightwatchman, to come with his key. If I should go to a concert or the theater, I would go with my mother or an aunt. I am not engaged to be married, so I have never had a date alone. No man would expect it of me, and I wouldn't want it. That is just our custom."

In many wealthy families, a *señorita de compania,* a full-time chaperone, is hired to watch over and escort society-aged daughters. Most girls, by preference and custom, put a guard over their own affairs; a girl may have many admirers or *pretendientes,* young men who express their interest in her through friends, admiring glances or polite letters, but usually only one *novio.* Spanish women, like all others, have the right to change their minds, but, in smaller villages, the girl who changes her *novio* sometimes loses respect in the eyes of her neighbors.

A young Spanish man explained it this way: "Love has great prestige here. In courtship, we usually have very pure, very idealistic relationships. In fact, with many Spanish girls, even a kiss is rare."

≪≪≪≪≪≪≪ ≫≫≫≫≫≫≫

In many parts of Spain, and especially in smaller towns, "courting habits" are so traditional that they fall into a definite pattern.

For instance, a young man may see a girl on the street whom he admires. To attract her attention, he may walk up and down in front of her house for several evenings, carrying a note to her in his hand. If she sees him and wants to meet him, she first gets her parents' permission, then sends a message through a friend that she will accept the note. This note usually asks that the boy be allowed to speak with her through the grilled windows of the house. (In small towns, most young people know each other well from childhood on, so this routine is merely romantic formality.)

Such through-the-grill conversations may be carried on, evening after evening, for weeks or until the parents of the girl find out all about the young man and are assured his intentions are honest. It is a marked step forward in the romantic relationship when the young man is asked into the house, to continue the visits under the watchful eyes of *madre y padre*. Only after a long but restrained friendship is the girl allowed to consider the young man her *novio*.

All through Spain, on the warm, flower-scented evenings, it is possible to see boys and girls standing for hours, talking at a window, doorway or front gate. This courtship—called "plucking the turkey" because it takes so long—may go on for six or seven years or until the girl is in her early twenties and the boy twenty-five or older. Few have money to marry earlier.

How do the Spanish teens and twenties react to these long, carefully watched-over courtships? Because it *is* their custom, most engaged couples adjust happily and enthusiastically to the months of *planning* together. They get to know each other thoroughly—not in the glamorous settings of country club dances, drive-in movies and beach barbecues, but in the down-to-earth settings of homes, with little children, kittens and future mother-in-laws sharing their friendship with them. The result is usually a realistic, stable and loving marriage.

Engagement rings are not often exchanged here but traditionally the *novio's* mother gives the *novia* a bracelet and the boy himself may give her small presents from time to time—a necklace, a fan or some perfume. Traditionally, too, the young man provides the parlor furniture to begin housekeeping; the girl is expected to furnish the bedroom and kitchen and bring with her all the linens for the house, usually carefully embroidered and handsewn. Even small households start life with drawers full of hand-hemmed linens that embody years of work. One village girl I know meticulously embroidered her new initials on everything, from bedsheets and handkerchiefs to aprons and bits of clean rag for kitchen scrub-ups! It was a labor of love that took her spare evenings for three or four years.

At most weddings, relatives and friends fill in the new household with small, useful gifts or sums of money. Of course, wealthy young brides begin their new lives with all the trimmings that money can buy. I knew one girl whose trousseau contained thirty-eight new dresses made by local *modistas!*

«««««« »»»»»»

Almost exclusively, weddings in Spain are held in Catholic churches and the ceremonies follow the rituals of that religion. One typical pre-wedding custom is purely social, yet almost as important to the bride as that sacred moment when she says "I do." This is the custom of visiting the bride at home, in the hour before she leaves for the church, to admire her and give felicitations and compliments. Even the poorest girl will save for years—or will rent for a day—an elaborate white wedding dress and veil. She will dress in her own home and wait there until the best man and the matron of honor call to escort her to church—where the groom is waiting. At home, friends and neighbors crowd in with exclamations of good fortune and admiration.

Recently, I went to the wedding of a friend who lived in one of the scattered rows of cottages along the beach. Outside her house, children and female neighbors stood six deep. Inside, the tiny front room was crowded. In the center stood the bride in a flowing gown of white patterned silk, held out by stiff petticoats. A thin lace veil covered her face and a chair stood behind her to hold the train of her dress away from the hard, mud-packed floor. Her dark hair was arranged in curls around the face, trembling hands, in white lace gloves, were folded tightly. She stood like a princess in a trance, tense with emotion, silently accepting the best wishes of friends. The church was about two miles distance and the crowd from the house trailed the bride to the wedding car. None of these people went to the church. They had, in a sense, helped to conduct a private ceremony at her house; they had come to admire the lovely bride and to join her in the dramatic moment when she left her own home as a single girl for the last time.

I knew the young bride very well, incidentally, and was aware that her total monthly earnings came to about fifteen dollars. What years of yearning, saving—and fine needlework—had gone into the splendor of her wedding day!

Later, the church ceremony was solemn; the party that followed was good-natured and gay; but the most dramatic time of all was the hour when the emotional, excited bride stood like a lost queen in her own mud-floored front room. Only one aspect of the religious marriage ceremony stands out in my mind as a "strange custom." Midway through the service, the priest looped a large, heavy cord lightly around the bride's shoulders, then around the groom's, linking them together. Fortunately, the cord was of braided white satin, so the symbolical "tying together" seemed graceful and right.

<<<<<<<<< >>>>>>>>>

Large receptions are held in clubs and hotels (or in big homes, of course) but often "budget" wedding parties spill out of tiny apartments or cottages right into the street. This is true of christening celebrations, too. Wine and cakes are served inside, but most of the dancing is done to a three-piece band or a pair of clicking castanets, right out on the cobblestoned road. Anyone may join the dancing crowd, but only an invited guest would step beyond the door.

<<<<<<<<< >>>>>>>>>

In the months of May and June, white-garbed children pop up all over the Spanish landscape, like fancy wax flowers. These are the boys and girls, usually about eight years old, who are going through the dramatic ceremony of making their First Holy Communion. Weeks of preparation in learning the Catholic catechism precede this significant day, so the children are mentally and spiritually prepared to accept its importance in their lives. Outwardly, they are dressed and ornamented as if for a lavish costume ball.

Little girls are usually gowned like miniature

brides in full, long-skirted white dresses, wax-pearl crowns, misty veils and white gloves. Some boys wear simple white shirts and short trousers but most are garbed in some variety of white sailor suit. The costuming seems to be *more* elaborate when the family has less money; a boy from a well-to-do family may have a classic sailor suit in white, while the family of a poorer boy will scrimp and save to buy him a long-trousered suit with a white coat, as lavishly epauletted and gold-braided as an admiral's dress uniform.

After the First Holy Communion services in church, the children have their pictures taken, then they either celebrate with a family party or wander through the streets or neighborhood with their parents—elaborate, petted and stared-at, little celebrities for the day. Some children are allowed to go from house to house, giving out illustrated Holy Cards in return for a peseta or two; others are promenaded up and down the main streets, catching the warm, affectionate smiles of passers-by, then pausing for lemonade or an ice cream in a sidewalk cafe.

Spanish children remember their First Communion day for its spiritual impact; many remember it also because they got so much extra attention.

«««««« »»»»»»

The Christmas season comes to Spain without any jingle bells, decorated fir trees or other red and green trimmings. Christmas Day is chiefly a family time, a day to go to Mass and to share a happy holiday dinner together. Gift-giving is postponed until

Spanish Customs · 59

the Feast of the Epiphany, on January 12th. These gifts are exclusively exchanged between intimate friends or family, however. Spain has never lured a Santa Claus or his counterpart across her borders.

Our mince pies and plum puddings are replaced on the Spanish holiday menu by a special Christmas cake, usually made of marzipan and candied fruits, in the shape of a fat, coiled serpent. Some serpent cakes come banquet size—big enough to serve dozens of people, while other serpents are coiled small enough for one family, but gay and colorful, with sugarplum eyes and stuck with fluffy pink or yellow feathers.

Turkeys are often served during the holiday season, but not the proud, crisp birds, roasted drumsticks up, that we are accustomed to seeing. In Spain, most turkeys are carefully boned before cooking, stuffed with sausage, chopped liver and hard-boiled eggs, then roasted and sliced at the table like some sort of edible basketball.

All over the country, the New Year is greeted with the same ritual: at the stroke of midnight, everyone eats twelve fresh grapes or raisins, to bring good luck for the twelve new months to come. This is usually followed by a little liquid grape, in the form of wine or brandy, to get the first day of the year off to a gay start.

«««««««« »»»»»»»»

Just as Macy's or Gimbel's begins to think of Christmas as soon as the Thanksgiving decorations are put away, so Christmas comes to Spain long before the month of December. "Christmas carolers"—Spanish fashion—come out about the third week of November. These are usually troops of little boys, all wearing big-brimmed straw hats hung with crepe-paper streamers and all playing a tambourine or a *bomba*. A *bomba* is an instrument that gives out a melancholy *"oomp-pa"* sound which echoes through the night like a bass horn or an outsized bullfrog. It is made from a clay flowerpot, tightly covered over the open end with a piece of thin goat skin. Through the center of the taut skin is stuck a long piece of cane. To play the *bomba,* the palm of the hand must be wet and then slid up and down the cane. This haunting sound, plus the jingling tambourines and high, wailing voices of the carolers, echoes through the pre-Christmas nights as the boys go from house to house or cafe to cafe, singing for *pesetas*. Sometimes older men go caroling for fun—claiming a glass of wine as a reward for each performance.

««««««« »»»»»»»

One of the most unusual customs in Spain is the presenting of "prayers" to the Blessed Virgin in the form of wax, plastic or silver shapes: a crippled leg, a baby's body, an oxen, a foot and other symbols. These "prayers" are hung in the church, near the statue of the Blessed Virgin, with the earnest hope that their nearness will remind her of the petitioner's special plea and persuade her to ask her Son to look with favor on the prayers for health, good crops or whatever it might be. The wax shapes, which discolor with age, often look like scraps from a bone yard, while the little silver "prayers," more graceful and durable, resemble pieces from a charm bracelet.

Besides asking for special favors, the devout Spaniards like to *thank* the Virgin for prayers answered through her intercession, so often they will present her with personal gifts — bracelets, rings, lockets, crowns and other valuables which then either adorn the statue or are placed nearby in glass cases. Of course, these gifts are not meant to flatter or bribe the Virgin; rather they are *sacrifices* intended to show that the donor is willing to give up something valued in appreciation for the Virgin's attention.

It is often strange to see a Virgin, into whose likeness the sculptor has put all the humility, kindness and simplicity associated with her, hung with worldly, incongruous rings, bracelets and earrings. But in their thinking, Spaniards endow the Mother of Christ with a very versatile and very human personality—with a woman's heart, she understands human suffering and, also with a woman's heart, she knows how difficult it is to give up a favorite necklace or jeweled tiarra.

<<<<<<<<< >>>>>>>>>

The practice of going into mourning is still widely followed throughout Spain and when a member of the family dies—from a child to grandparents — all female members of the family wear only black for a full year. Male members of the family remember the dead by wearing black bands sewed onto coat or shirt sleeves. Sometimes, when mourning periods overlap, women may find themselves in mourning for years on end and, in some cases—since a complete change of wardrobe is expensive—it becomes easier simply to wear black at all times. Many country women, over thirty or forty, wear nothing else.

Since death is a natural and inevitable thing, every death should not necessarily bring long periods of sorrow. Yet in Spain, tradition and custom are strong. For instance, it is against tradition to marry within a year after a parent or grandparent's death. This can play havoc with young lives. We knew a girl who had planned to be married in about three months' time and all preparations were made. Suddenly, her eighty-five-year-old grandmother became ill. Knowing the strength of tradition in the village, the grandmother herself urged that the wedding take place at once. She lived to see her beloved granddaughter in her wedding dress, sat propped up in a chair during the post-wedding festivities—and died about ten days later, having given her granddaughter a true gift of love.

<<<<<<<<< >>>>>>>>>

On Palm Sunday, as it happens in Catholic churches all over the world, Mass-goers are presented with sprays of blessed palms in memory of Jesus Christ's triumphal entrance into Jerusalem. In Spain, most of the palms come from a certain town in the south called Elche. After Easter, these palms are twisted into the second-floor balcony railings, to bring blessings to that house for the year. Little blessed crosses of woven palm are used to decorate the bridles of donkeys and work cows on the farms.

«««««««« »»»»»»»»

St. John's Day or Midsummer's Eve is supposedly a night of magic and soothsaying, celebrated in rural areas by fig-eating expeditions; groups of young people go out to gather and eat fresh figs after dark, making special wishes. On this evening, too, girls may make love tests: tear a fig leaf and, if the break heals overnight, one's true love will be found. Gather two shoots of wild artichokes and put them outside a window. If they have flowered by morning, true love will be serene. Spin a needle on the surface of a saucer of water. If it stays afloat, the boy to whom it points will be a love for life.

Obviously, young Spaniards—like most lovers in the world—find a touch of trouble stimulating to affection, since none of the tests can possibly bring positive results!

«««««««« »»»»»»»»

Paseo, in translation, means simply "walk," and the Spaniards are the greatest pleasure walkers in the world. The *paseo* is a social affair, a promenade for exercise, chatting and greeting friends. *Novios* and *novias* or whole families like to take a leisurely stroll up a main street, or through the park, early in the evening, before the dinner hour. Mothers like to dress children in their pastel best for these walks and every attractive girl grooms herself as if she were going to an important party. On Sunday or holiday evenings, whole towns come alive, with well-groomed, affable citizens filling the streets. At ten o'clock on a Sunday evening, traffic is almost stopped in small villages because pedestrians spill out onto the road!

Next to *walking* in the *paseo,* the next most popular relaxation is *watching* the *paseo.* A cup of coffee or a sherry at a sidewalk cafe entitles a Spaniard to an hour or so of restful leisure to watch the parade.

One night in Cadiz, an old town with narrow, house-walled streets, we left the hotel ourselves for a stroll and were drawn to a great noise a few blocks away. We expected a carnival or a street fiesta but it was only the sounds of the crowd on a *paseo* street, walking five and six abreast, making a chatter that rose above the houses and echoed for blocks around.

I was amused also to notice that in Tetuan, a town in old Spanish Morocco, in the north of Africa, the Moslems, in spite of their traditional seclusion for women, had picked up the Spanish *paseo* habit. In the twilight, married Moslem couples sauntered arm-in-arm, the women carefully veiled but nevertheless out taking the air, just like their Spanish neighbors.

<<<<<<<<< >>>>>>>>>

A curious phrase, **sin vergüenza,** governs much of Spanish behavior. It is a phrase which means "without shame" but it suggests a more positive injunction—"with pride." In the Spanish code, it is a disgrace to behave *sin vergüenza*, or without pride in such things as good manners, good appearance, consideration for others and so on. Examples of those persons *sin vergüenza,* might be a man who lets himself be seen under the influence of wine, a girl who walks too boldly in the village street, a housewife who nags in public or shouts at her children; in short, anyone who is not *caballero* or mannerly in his behavior.

Because of this feeling, some of the most elegant manners, the best postures, the warmest greetings and the most loyal friendships exist in Spain. To be *sin vergüenza* is to fail as a good Spaniard. In this country, every man likes to think well of himself. The people are like actors and actresses, determined to be attractive on a stage, no matter how small their parts. And to be truly *caballero,* the heart should be as graceful and attractive as the body, never *sin vergüenza.*

Chapter V

FAMOUS SPANIARDS

THE SPAIN of today and the many Spains of yesterday have produced numerous outstanding men and women, personalities whose names ring out clearly down the long hallways of history—names that were great in war, names that were great in art, literature, religion and the sciences.

Some of these people have become "world names" now, so well known that one hardly remembers that they *are* Spaniards, people who first saw daylight in some white-walled Spanish cottage or some chilly castle on a rocky Iberian Coast.

Here, looking backward from famous Spaniards living today to those now entombed in history books, are sketches of just a few of the well-known men and women who called this country of mountains and orange groves *mi patria,* "my fatherland."

⟪⟪⟪⟪⟪⟪⟪⟪ ⟫⟫⟫⟫⟫⟫⟫⟫

Salvador Dali: The bright pop-eyes, sharp wax mustaches and sleekly eccentric appearance of this surrealist artist often make him look as "out of this world" as his famous paintings of green sunsets, limp clocks and half-fried eggs. Dali, at home now in world capitals from New York to Paris, was born in Madrid.

〈〈〈〈〈〈〈〈〈 〉〉〉〉〉〉〉〉〉

Pablo Picasso: The dazzling blue of the Mediterranean, the clear yellow of sunlight, the cashmere color of mountains in fall—has the appreciation of color so evident in the work of artist Picasso anything to do with his birthplace and the sights he first saw as a child? Perhaps so, because Picasso was born in Malaga, on the southernmost coast of Spain, not far from Africa. His father taught later at the Academy of Fine Arts in Barcelona and gave Pablo his first instructions in art. Most people today think of Picasso as a Frenchman, partly because he influenced so many French painters. But Picasso first crossed the border Pyrenees as a nineteen-year-old student; since his early twenties he has made France his home. Yet Spaniards will not give up Pablo Picasso as "one of ours"; they are quick to remind tourists and art lovers that this painter of such famous works as *The Tragedy* and *The Acrobats* came from their peninsula. In fact, Picasso's sister still lives in a cluttered apartment in Malaga, a constant target for art students and culture-minded travelers who call to ask if they may look at the room where famous Brother Pablo first set up his easel.

〈〈〈〈〈〈〈〈〈 〉〉〉〉〉〉〉〉〉

Pablo Casals: Another Pablo, another story. This renowned violincellist, one of our greatest living musicians and now an old man of eighty-three was born near Barcelona and studied there and in Madrid. It was not until he was successful in Paris and London, however, that the Spaniards recognized a genius of their own. Yet for nearly a quarter of a century, Casals has not set foot on his native soil. A strong freedom-lover, he is now an exile who has vowed never to return to Spain until Generalissimo Franco's regime is ended. His music is sweet to the rest of the world, but Spain no longer hears it.

«««««« »»»»»»»

Generalissimo Francisco Franco: This tough little soldier, now in his late sixties, has been the stern, one-man ruler of Spain since shortly after 1936. At that date, he was head of the Spanish Foreign Legion forces. When civil war broke out in Spain, Franco was stationed in Africa. Quick to see political and military opportunity, he rounded up the Spanish troops on that continent, re-routed them to Spain and served as their military leader until the end of the war, in 1939.

This is a simple summary of one of the hardest, saddest wars ever fought—brother against brother, village against village. An anguished Spain settled down to recovery with the General as its leader. In 1947, Franco was confirmed as head of the state for life and given the right to name his successor. Today, he runs a tight country, with strict control of the military and civil services, plus heavy censorship of newspapers and radio.

An old friend of mine, a Spanish Marques who

served with Franco during the war and knows him well, describes the General as a serious, hearty, unsubtle man, with little humor and scant time for amusements. He has been married for many years to a wife who, in Spanish style, stays somewhat in the background; their only child is now the wife of a Spanish nobleman. His personal habits are still soldierly: early rising, long work hours, simple diet, strict personal discipline. His soldierly indulgences are a rough-tough vocabulary, a rare glass of spirits and an occasional all-night card game with the boys.

Though pictures of Franco adorn every shop and public building in Spain, he is not a show-off dictator who likes to display himself at rallies and parades as did Tito of Jugoslavia or Peron of Argentina in their days of power. In my many visits to Spain, I was able to glimpse Franco in person only once—in his special box at a bullfight. On this occasion he was carefully nonmilitary, without a guard or a uniformed man in sight. The Generalissimo wore a conservative business suit without medals and had the prosperous, well-groomed air of a vice president on the way to the bank. The reaction of the crowd was polite, but definitely cool. They rose, cheering, as Franco entered his box. But the voices were raised only in minimum courtesy. The Generalissimo acknowledged the ovation briefly, then waved for the *corrida* to begin. Dictators and their accompanying military displays are simply not popular any more—and Franco is smart enough to change his approach to the people accordingly.

Do the Spaniards *like* living under a dictator—do

they *like* Franco? Such questions would probably bring a nod of indifference from most Spaniards. The Generalissimo is a strong ruler who took hold when the country was weak; he keeps all opposition strictly under control. What can be changed *now,* what can the individual Spaniard do but shrug?

Many Spaniards, however, are truly and strongly pro-Franco. They believe he is a valiant soldier who saved their country from the more terrible enemy: Communism. Some feel that a dictator government that keeps peace is better than a free government that leads to war.

A newspaperman once explained his attitude to me this way: "At the end of the terrible Civil War we were a destroyed country. We were like a man with a broken leg. Franco is our healing cast. He has held us together in our convalescence."

<<<<<<<<< >>>>>>>>>

Manolete: The man Manuel Rodrigez, known as "Manolete," must be *explained?* Few Spaniards would believe this possible. Surely, they would protest, the fame of this man, the greatest of all matadors, must have found its way around the world. When he died in the little white infirmary of the bullring in Linares, on August 29, 1947, all Spain went into shocked mourning. And today, every bullfighter, living and dead, is still compared to the great Manolete.

Until his fatal goring, Manolete had fought more bravely and more gracefully than any man ever to face the giant horn-spread of a Miura bull. Every time he entered a bullring, his skill—plus some extra mysterious quality—brought crowds of *aficionados* to their feet in screaming praise. The mysterious quality was partly a brooding, fatalistic charm that made each appearance seem tensely significant. Manolete was in his twenties when he died. Many Spaniards insist he knew he was destined to die in the bull arena, under a blazing Spanish sky, hence the melancholy, tortured look, the air of patient waiting. Others say he suffered from tuberculosis and hence faced a possible double death every time he fought—the sharp horns of the bull and the strain on his troubled lungs.

I never saw Manolete, of course, but I have watched many films of his *corridas*. He was a slight, muscular man, with a craggy face and dark, brooding eyes. His body was one of power and energy, but there was a great sadness in even his most graceful movements. Whatever thoughts actually passed through his head, he projected as a polished tragedian, an actor whose very presence brought a hush of awe over his audience. Perhaps his own foreboding of death was so great that it touched everyone who watched him.

In Cordoba, the town of his birth, stands a museum built to honor this great matador. Here, in carefully shined glass cabinets are the blood-stiffened garments he wore that last day in the ring; here too are his capes and favorite *trajes de luces,* the bright, gold-traced garments worn by bullfighters. In the center room, almost as in a church shrine, lies an excellently sculptured figure of Manolete as he lay in death, hands folded, shadowed, hollowed eyes closed in peace. The sculptor skillfully marked the left cheek with a lifelike duplicate of the clefting scar once made by a bull. But that gray cheek is now worn smooth. In death, Manolete's devoted fans kissed away his marble wound.

«««««««« »»»»»»»»

Miguel de Cervantes: Who is the most famous of all Spanish writers? Miguel de Cervantes, poet, dramatist and novelist, a man born over four hundred years ago. Yet today—after the passing of more than three centuries—Spaniards are pleased to acknowledge him as their prime writing genius and his literary characters are so well-known that little carved statuettes of the knobby, lean-ribbed horse, Rosinante from *Don Quixote,* are sold in stalls and gift shops as commonly as Americans might peddle Mickey Mouses.

Cervantes showed himself in history first as a soldier, fighting bravely at the Battle of Lepanto, even though, it is recorded, he had a high fever and subsequently received three gunshot wounds, one of which permanently maimed his left hand. A few years later, a warship on which he was serving was seized by Barbary pirates. Cervantes was captured and held as a slave in Algiers for nearly five years, while his family negotiated and tried to raise ransom.

It was not until he returned to Spain and was rejected for several civil service jobs that he desperately turned to writing. He married then—for love, perhaps, but not for money, as it is noted that his wife's dowry consisted of nothing more than "five vines, an orchard, some household furniture, four beehives, 45 hens and chickens, one cock and a crucible."

During a long period of literary production, culminating with *Don Quixote,* written when he was in his middle fifties, Cervantes was constantly harassed for money and finally died an old but very poor celebrity. His work has outlived many changes in literary taste and is even more popular now than it was during his lifetime. Great talent is often paid off in odd ways, however. Today, every second donkey in Spain answers to the nickname "Rosinante." Perhaps, with his wry humor, Cervantes might feel this humble memory is honor enough.

<<<<<<<<< >>>>>>>>>

Saint Ignatius of Loyola: a wealthy young Spaniard, handsome, strong-willed, impetuous, a soldier and man of the world. This was the young Ignatius of Loyola, born in a castle in the province of Guipuzcoa, just a year before Columbus discovered America.

In his thirtieth year, a great change came over Ignatius, a spiritual revolution which started him on the laborious, self-torturing journey to sainthood. In a military battle with the French at Navarre, he was severely wounded and in the painful months of convalescence he found himself dreaming of a certain *señorita* with whom he was infatuated—and struggling with a new turn of his thoughts. The vision of his lady love grew blurred as he became concerned with his own soul. On his sickbed, Ignatius read first a *Life of Christ* and then a book called *Flowers of the Saints;* he was swept with a vast guilt for his past sins and a strong determination to find the best way in this life to serve God.

Once his war wound healed, Ignatius showed his body no mercy. At one point, he gave away all his rich clothing and possessions and retired to a cave, where he prayed seven hours a day, scourged himself three times daily and emaciated his body with fasting. In the years that followed, he studied at various universities and finally, having honed himself into a tool of great spiritual strength, he and several devout companions obtained Papal permission to found the Society of Jesus, known more commonly in the United States as the Jesuit Order.

There have been many outstanding Jesuit explorers in the past. Today, the Jesuits are recognized chiefly as excellent and exacting teachers, with schools for young men and student priests in most parts of the world. The lonely meditations of a love-sick Spanish soldier gave the Catholic world some of its best teachers—and Spain its greatest saint.

《《《《《《《《 》》》》》》》》

Torquemada: In a country of *many* contrasts such as Spain, one is bound to find contrast also in religion—and religious personalities. Ignatius of Loyola and Torquemada were both deeply pious men but—well, here is the story of Torquemada.

Did you know that today there are almost no persons of the Jewish faith or lineage in Spain? This strange condition leads back to Thomas Torquemada, the son of a Spanish nobleman, who was born in Valladolid almost five hundred fifty years ago. While Ignatius sought to discipline and educate himself, then teach others, Torquemada chose to confuse religion with terror.

Young Thomas joined the Friars Preachers (Dominican), took his vows and studied philosophy and theology extensively. As his religious career progressed, he was noted for his wisdom and his zeal. At one point, the famous Queen Isabella chose him as her confessor; later her husband, Ferdinand, decided that he too would confide his sins and seek advice from this particular man of God. Torquemada himself, in spite of his high position in court, stayed simple; he did not want honors or special ecclesiastical position. He only wanted power and he got it.

One must remember that this was the Middle Ages, when wars were often fought for personal whim and such flimsy excuses as "personal honor." It was also a time when religious feeling ran high. Besides this, powerful, Catholic Spain was only a boat ride from Africa and the anti-Christian faith of the Moslems. Also, in the eyes of Torquemada, his beloved country was being overrun and undermined by Jews. Many Jews and Moslems, either receiving a true gift of faith or for reasons of personal security, *did* become Catholics—but Torquemada was still worried.

After consultation with Isabella and Ferdinand, and with the permission of Pope Sixtus IV in Rome, Torquemada set up an Inquisition. This was, in great brief, "an ecclesiastical tribunal for the suppression of heresy and the punishment of heretics." During the lifetime of Isabella alone, the Inquisition resulted in the execution of 2,000 persons—Jews, Moslems and any people whose true Catholicity was doubted—for such various crimes as heresy, witchcraft, bigamy, usury, black magic, etc. History suggests, too, that some unfortunates were executed by powerful rivals simply for the sake of revenge, or in order that their rich businesses and fertile farm lands might be confiscated. The trials were accompanied by tortures and injustices that have made the phrase "Spanish Inquisition" a dark one in history.

I myself am repelled by *any* contemplation of physical tortures or cruelty but I read with appreciative interest an account of one of these group trials in H. V. Morton's *Stranger in Spain*. It is excellent for its accuracy, color and clear understanding of the times.

However, even the purges of the Inquisition did not put Torquemada's mind at ease about his religion or his country. As adviser to the Crown, he undoubtedly influenced Ferdinand and Isabella when, in 1492, they issued an edict banning all unconverted Jews from Spain. It is estimated that 200,000 Jews fled before this law.

Spaniards today deplore the Inquisition and the excesses of those times and would like them to be forgotten, just as we feel alarm and shame at the witchcraft trials that once took place in our own country.

Why mention Torquemada at all, a man whose Christian drives were distorted so they eliminated the all-important virtues basically taught in Christianity—kindness, compassion and a true love for one's fellow man? Because Torquemada is an important historical part of Spain and the effects of his "work" are still felt in Spain today. There are many Spaniards who feel their current economic picture might be painted in stronger, more cheerful colors if a Jewish influence had remained in the country to help through the centuries with the activities of day-to-day business.

<<<<<<<<< >>>>>>>>>

Isabella, Queen of Spain: Isabella, 'La Catolica,' is Spain's most famous queen, a brilliant woman, personally fine and honest, who lives in the eyes of the "new" world chiefly as the Benefactress who made it possible for Christopher Columbus to sail for America.

Although Queen Isabella is given great credit for her foresight in backing Columbus' momentous voyage, it actually took her six years to make up her mind. The Queen was first told of Columbus' daring plans after he had tried to get financial backing from both France and Portugal. But at that date (1486), Spain was engaged in a bitter war to free its lands from Moorish conquerors. Ultimately, Spain was victorious and, in January, 1492, Queen Isabella finally had the time, and the money, to talk business with Christopher Columbus. She received him at the graceful, ornate Moorish palace, the Alhambra, in the hill city of Granada, in southern Spain. As do most tourists, we visited the room in the palace where Columbus supposedly fell on his knees in gratitude before Her Majesty. Today, the intricate, lacy archways and the colored tile traceries are as polished and scrubbed clean as they must have been on that historic day. The tinkling fountains still play through the cool rooms.

But the triumph of victory over the Moors did not make Isabella a softhearted or foolish ruler. Columbus, in this interview, demanded high terms. He asked for the immediate rank of admiral, "Admiral of the Ocean" in all seas, islands and continents he might discover, plus a tenth of the precious metals discovered within his admiralty. His terms were refused. In fact, the rebuff was so final that he actually left town but a messenger from the Queen caught up with him about six miles outside Granada. Terms were finally reached. Isabella became so enthusiastic she volunteered to pawn her jewels if the state treasury could not raise funds, and a short time later Columbus sailed out from the Spanish coast and straight into American history.

For all her power, strength and good works, plus the support of a loyal husband, Isabella lived a life darkened frequently by human tragedy. Several of her children died in childhood and her oldest, much-loved daughter lived out a gloomy existence as *Juana la Loca,* Joan the Mad, an equally promising, talented woman whom Middle Ages' medicine could not cure of growing mental illness. The life of Queen Isabella was not always pomp and glory; there were many tears and little white crosses along the way.

≪≪≪≪≪≪≪≪ ≫≫≫≫≫≫≫≫

The Three Painters: Spain in the Middle Ages produced almost as many great artists as did Italy in the same period—men of true genius whose canvasses fill museums, churches and private collections through half the earth. Out of this roster of talent, here are just *three* great artists, each in his way a special example of "Spanish art."

El Greco: This man was born Domenicos Theotocopoulos, on the island of Crete, in the mid-sixteenth century. Though he signed his work "El Greco," The Greek, he is Spanish through and through. He came to Spain as a young man, via Italy, and the house and studio in which he did much of his work still stands in Toledo, about forty-four miles out of Madrid. Here alone are El Greco paintings valued at three million dollars.

During the first stages of his work, El Greco—like other painters of his day throughout Europe—

was busy searching for a patron among royalty or high ecclesiastics who might commission or support him in his career. His first major work in Toledo was done expressly for the cathedral there. Impressed by the great canvas, "The Stripping of Christ Before the Crucifixion," Philip II asked the artist to do an altarpiece for *his* pet piece of architecture, the ambitious and melancholy mausoleum, El Escorial. Most of El Greco's early masterpieces are strongly religious in theme; later he did some striking portraits of contemporary Spaniards.

His genius was recognized well within his lifetime, and he was praised with both fame and money. At his death, he lived in a twenty-four-room suite in the palace of a Toledian Marques, his windows overlooking the brown River Tagus. El Greco produced a tremendous amount of work in his lifetime and his longheaded, richly colored figures are recognizable at a glance in galleries everywhere. The famous Prado Museum in Madrid displays walls lined with his work and, in many small-town churches, proud guides lead tourists to gaze up at an El Greco hung dimly above an ornate altar. Spain permeated El Greco and El Greco permeated Spain. To me, El Greco will always be associated not with well-lit museums or even the crooked, geranium-bright streets around his studio in Toledo but with the dusty light and odors of worn leather and snuffed candles that hang over closed cathedrals.

Velazquez: Though this son of an aristocratic family, born to a lawyer and his wife in Seville in

1599, has a five-part name, he is best known by the signature on his paintings: Velazquez. He is generally considered to be one of the greatest painters the world has ever known.

Velazquez was a grand-scale yet intimate painter, catching physical and color details, plus variations of the human face, as accurately as a camera, yet with imagination. This technique was deliberate and he started his early self-training by painting minutely simple things: earthenware jugs, fruit, fish and flowers. At one point, he hired a peasant boy as servant-companion-model and did charcoal sketches of his face a thousand times and more, to catch a thousand different expressions.

Married young and with two children, Velazquez came to Madrid at twenty-five and received instant favor at the Court. King Philip became his patron and friend for the next thirty-six years. We often hear that "today's youth is too security-minded." Well, here is the "security" Velazquez asked for and got as court painter: a monthly salary, lodgings, medical attendance and a special fee for any pictures he might paint. Later, a "clothing and travel" allowance was added.

His paintings range in subject from Christianity to mythology, and most memorable are his portraits, biographies on canvas, showing the costumes, customs, pomps and characters of the court and times in which he lived. It is like looking at illustrated history. Velazquez loved the droll dwarfs and buffoons that were popular in court life in his day, and they frequent his pictures. One of the most famous masterpieces hangs in a special room in the Prado, in Madrid. It is called *"Las Meninas"* (The Maids of Honor) and shows a little princess at play, surrounded by young attendants and with Velazquez painting in the background. Staring out from the foreground of the canvas is a youngish female dwarf, stunted but attractively gowned, soft-faced, quizzical and very appealing.

Today, in order to give proper appreciation to the color and perspective of this painting, the canvas is hung on one wall of a special room so it is reflected, unframed, in a huge mirror in another corner. Now, I had read the history of the picture, plus accounts of its unusual hanging in the museum, yet at first sight I was both startled and unbelievably awed. Seeing the mirrored painting, I stopped short, embarrassed. So intimate, so realistic and so alive is the little dwarf in the foreground that I thought I had bumped into a living child! And yet that quiet scene of palace life was put on canvas over three hundred years ago.

Francisco Goya: The early life of this rough-tough genius reads a little like the story of a present-day beatnik—one who made good. He was born in 1749, in the town of Saragossa, a poor boy and an unpredictable one. At nineteen, because of a street fight in which three youths were killed, he found it wise to leave his home town and move on to Madrid. Though less homicidal, his time in Madrid was troublesome enough to persuade Goya that he should move on again, and he worked his way to the east coast of Spain as one of a group of itinerant bullfighters. He finally arrived in Rome, broke and ill, and stayed on long enough to rebuild his health and fit in four years of art study. This teen-twenty phase of his existence gave him an intimate knowledge of life from slum streets to barrooms and bullfighting that shows itself clearly in some of Goya's best work.

As time and talent progressed, he became a favorite portrait painter with the current court, although most of his portraits are realistically cruel, unflattering and accurate, showing the decadence that weak wills, intermarriage and general dissolution had brought to the Spanish royal family. Goya was a fast and facile worker, often taking only two or three hours to finish a portrait. In brief, he was an excellent reporter-on-canvas, and shows vigorously what the life and people of Spain were like in his time. Some of Goya's war canvasses are the most terrifying and explicit antiwar propaganda ever painted.

Goya died at eighty-four, almost totally deaf, but painting once again his "simple friends," the people around him, as he had in his first artistic days. Some of his last pictures are called "The Milkmaid," "The Water Carrier" and "The Knife Grinder." To the very end, the "little boy of the streets" kept his work strong, earthy and pulsing with the life of Spain.

«««««« »»»»»»

Spanish conquistadors: The flap of sail, the roll of military drums and the clash of swords is background music to the dozens of stories of Spaniards in the New World. Two little boys, destined to become great explorers in the name of the Spanish throne, were born in the territory of Estramadura, just ten years apart—nearly five hundred years ago.

Vasco Nunez de Balboa was the older, born in 1475 to wealthy, educated parents. In his late youth, he became an unsuccessful farmer, piling up debts so enormous that historical rumor suggests he first shipped out to sea—and on his way to the discovery of the Pacific—"hidden in a barrel of victuals." Balboa was a kind-hearted conqueror, known for his bravery, courtesy and just dealings with those he met in new territories. But his life was touched with peaks of glory, valleys of hardship—and finished by death in disgrace. At one point, in honor of the discovery of the "great South sea" or Pacific Ocean, he was heralded in Spain as a national hero and Ferdinand the Catholic appointed him Admiral, with other grants and authorities, of the "new waters." Just three years later, a rival Spaniard falsely accused Balboa of treason and he was executed in a public square at the sad young age of forty-two. In this manner, Spain said *good-by* and *thank you* to one of its greatest explorers.

The second youth, *Hernando Cortes*, was a member of Balboa's troupe of 190 Spaniards on the momentous day when the Pacific was first sighted and claimed for the Spanish flag. His career ranged from student to farmer to conqueror, for he studied law at the great University of Salamanca and worked as

Pictures through the courtesy of the Spanish Tourist Office

Here is a typical plaza, the heart of every village or big-city neighborhood. Cool shade for resting, a tinkling fountain—and old friends to chat with.

Soon these flooded rice paddies outside Valencia will sprout a brilliant green. Here a farm worker surf-boards over surface to cultivate rich, black soil. Horses as work-beasts are both expensive and rare.

An early morning catch is hauled from the Mediterranean outside Malaga. Fishing methods are centuries old and rough seas make work difficult. But men and boys toil side by side to eke out meager daily rations.

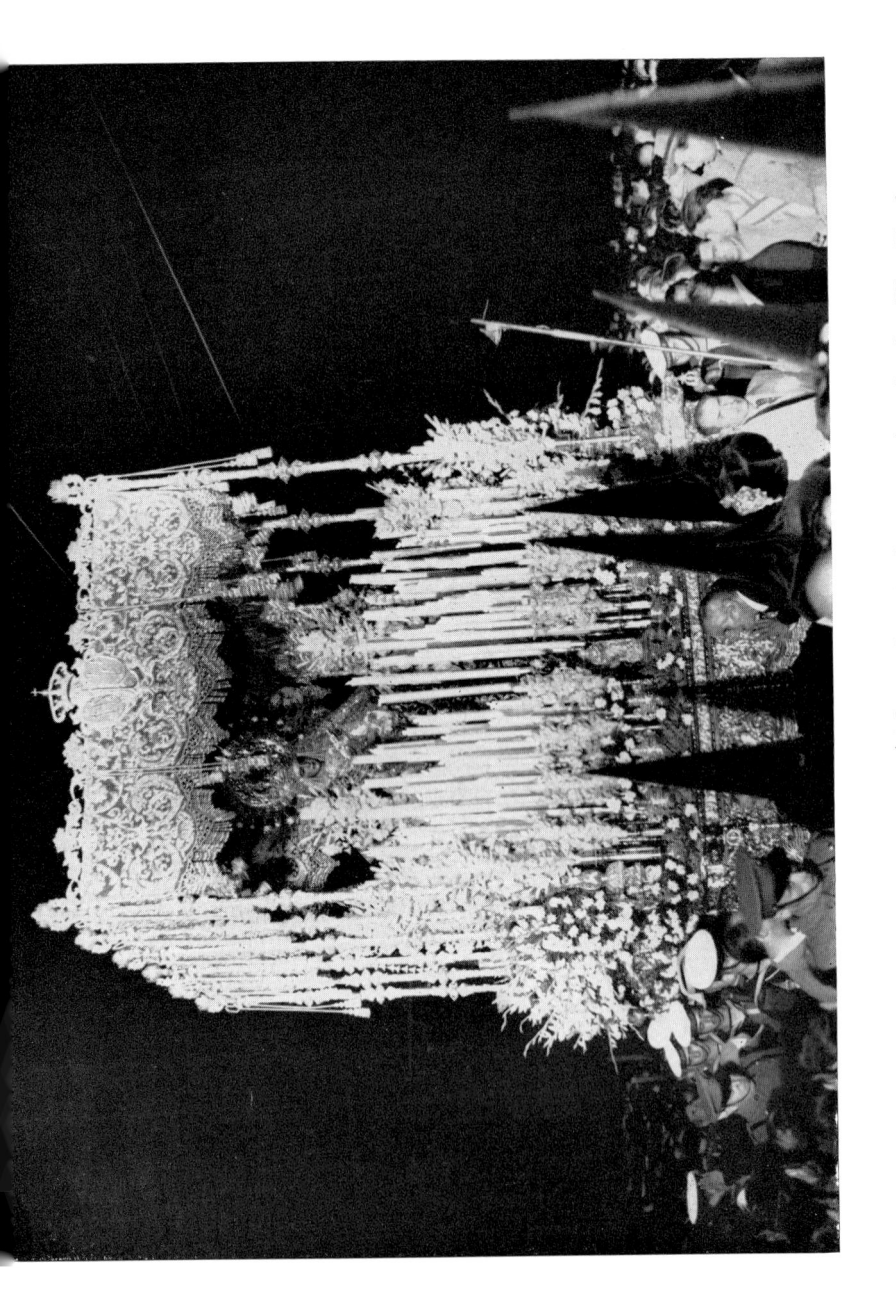

Solemnity and splendor spark this Holy Week procession in Seville. Each parish sends out its statue of the Virgin, jeweled and decked as the Queen

Triana celebrates a holiday—the "name day" of the town saint. Silken shawls draped from balconies are family treasures, brought out only for special occasions; straw blinds keep out hot sun, persistent flies.

Simple village street in southern Spain with rough, cobbled walks and white-washed houses. Barred windows keep out more cats than thieves. Inner courtyards make airy summer quarters, a-blaze with flowers.

Every day is wash-day in rural Spain. This matron in the central province of Leon is carrying a load to local stream. Roman ruins still stand nearby.

Sunlight, sand, brave matadors and applauding crowds. This is the great bullfight spectacle. Horses are thickly padded to prevent injury.

Modern farm equipment is rare in country Spain. Giant work cows, a special breed, pull wagons on rural roads, heads masked against the summer sun.

"Sounds of Christmas music" for sale in city market. Tambourines are made of goatskin and bits of tin; crown-topped *bombas* sound like big bullfrogs.

Flamenco, the gypsy-born dance of Spain, rings with sound, swirls with movement. Dancers stamp feet, clap hands to point up wild, staccato rhythms.

At Cordoba, red and white striped arches fill the famed mosque-cathedral, a union of two religious architectures. Surrounding orange groves scent the air.

The tower, *La Giralda,* in Seville is built upon the remains of a Moorish mosque. Tower was built in 12th century, is famous for swinging brass bell.

These Gothic towers, pitted with time, have survived since Middle Ages. Modern Barcelona is a gay port city, little-sister to sophisticated Madrid.

At the graceful Court of the Lions in the Alhambra, 124 white marble columns support intricate fret-work arches constructed by old Moorish craftsmen.

The intersection of the Calle Alcala and the Cibeles Fountain in beautiful, busy Madrid. The Gran Via branches off to the right in the background.

a farmer and notary before setting sail for the new world—and the ultimate conquering of Mexico. His fierce bravery, his cruelty in battle and his betrayal of the Aztec chief, Montezuma, are familiar to American students from their fourth grade history books on. More detailed accounts of his work in Mexico show him as a farsighted, thoughtful conqueror, who tried hard to improve the government, organize and increase agricultural production and develop the resources of the land. But the greed and jealousy of the Spanish court in the homeland played against him. He was recalled to Spain but no assignment was found for him there. He died just outside the town of Seville, but the imprint of his Spanish touch was left forever on distant Mexico.

Chapter VI

TEEN-AGED PROFILES—SEÑORITA Y SEÑOR

A HANDSHAKE, a kiss on the cheek, a stiff bow from the waist—what would it be like to meet a Spanish teen-ager in person? As a traveler, I made friends with many young Spaniards. As a reporter, I decided to pick out two special young people, a boy and a girl, ask them questions, get to know their families, watch their daily activities— and then put the bits and pieces of their lives on paper until I had their profiles down in black and white. Now they are ready for introductions.

These two people are the same age, live in the same city—but what different pictures their profiles show. Perhaps you would like to meet first "the silhouette with the rose in her hair," Aracelis Barrionuevo-Bolin.

<<<<<<<<< >>>>>>>>>

From the noises alone, you could guess that you are in Spain. As you stand on the broad stone steps of Bella Vista, No. 40, palm trees swish overhead,

Teen-aged Profiles · 87

an old street car clatters by on a narrow track and the tick-tack of donkeys' hoofs sound in the streets. From behind the house comes the great, rhythmic crash of the waves of the blue Mediterranean and in a nearby garden a thin, sweet voice sings out a gypsy song.

It is a late afternoon, and the hot summer sun is beating down on the old seaside city of Malaga. As you look up, you see that every window is shuttered tight against the heat and even the potted geraniums on the balconies droop a little. Once again, you lift the big brass door knocker, shaped like a clenched fist, and the knock echoes through the three-story white stone house. Suddenly, the door is swung open by a little maid in a clean cotton uniform. Inside, the house is dark and cool but your welcome is warm and almost overwhelming.

Not only is sixteen-year-old Aracelis on hand to greet you but her whole family of seventeen other persons as well.

School is out for the summer and the offices in busy Malaga are keeping nine to one o'clock summer hours. Practically all the Barrionuevos are at home: Aracelis, her parents, five of her six brothers and sisters, her seventy-three-year-old grandmother, five assorted cousins who live with them and three housemaids, plus an old nurse named Eloisa—she had been with Señora Barrionuevo since the day *she* was born—who serves the household as a hardworking, cheerful "extra grandmother." Only the oldest daughter is not at home. She was married last year, at nineteen, thus leaving Aracelis the oldest child in this bustling, chattering home where eighteen people sit down to every meal.

"Most Spaniards have big families," says Aracelis with a shy smile, "so I am used to crowds. It would be even busier if you'd come on a day when the 'powdered milks' were around." The "powdered milks" (baby food) is the nickname for a crowd of teen-aged boys and girls who like to spend their afternoons and early evenings together, dancing, swimming, or visiting from house to house.

"In the wintertime," her father told me, "this house is very tranquil. The children all go to school and, in the evening, they must all do their studies. But in the summertime, I think we must be heard in Africa!" Malaga is a Mediterranean port town and the Barrionuevo house, set in an elegant, old-family neighborhood, opens its back door right onto the stony beach. Directly across the sea lies the northern coast of Africa.

In some ways, Aracelis seems much older than sixteen, in some ways much younger. Like many Spanish girls, she is exceptionally pretty and well-groomed, although she wears simple clothes and no make-up except a touch of lipstick. Her hair is shaped in a neat page-boy without a bobby pin in sight; her manner is calm and poised and she behaves with the great courtesy with which every Spaniard seems to be born.

But in spite of her sophisticated appearance, she is babied and protected by her parents. They know where she is and what she is doing in work hours and play hours, and she is watched over like some rare, fragile jewel. "She is so young," Señora Barrionuevo is likely to murmur from time to time.

"But I *am* a working girl now," Aracelis would be quick to explain to you. "Last year—after five years of hard studies—I finished my courses at La Ascencion, a convent school for girls here in Malaga, like a high school. Then I went up to Madrid and got my "social service" certificate in only two months of study. The time went fast because I had already learned to do most of the things at home!"

Because I was a stranger, Aracelis paused to explain the "social service" certificate to me. Spain has been a dictator country since long before she was born: for twenty-three years, since the end of the Spanish Civil War, Generalissimo Franco has been the strong head of the State. Aracelis has read about democracy but she has never lived in a completely free country.

"Franco likes Spanish girls to be well-educated," she explains. "He likes us all to know something about the arts and also about cooking, sewing, taking care of the house and babies—and something about our country and government. So all girls are asked to go for some time to a state-run social service school—just like Spanish boys go to the army for eighteen months. Only our time is much shorter.

"At school, we all wear simple blouse-and-skirt uniforms, and all types of girls study together. We each pay about fifty cents a day for our board. My school was outside Madrid, almost across the road from Franco's summer palace."

One item about teen-aged life in a dictator country, Aracelis did not mention to me: this "social service certificate," a sign of indoctrination in a state school, is very important to young Spanish girls. Without it, no one may get a passport or be assigned government or civil service work. Indoctrination buys privileges. Also, since the State does not pay train fare for such trips, many poorer girls never get to the social service schools at all.

Little by little, the smaller children of the family drifted to play in other rooms. Downstairs in the big house, all the floors are scrubbed red brick and the walls a cool gray. In the front hall is a chipped Roman bust dating from around 600 A.D.; a friend of the Barrionuevo's plowed it up on a nearby farm, a relic of the ancient times when the Romans colonized Spain. In the living and dining rooms hang giant mirrors with carved gilt frames, brought from Venice many years ago by wealthy relatives. Hung in the small front hall is a startlingly modern Picasso print, simply framed. "We are proud of Picasso," explains Aracelis. "He was born right here in Malaga, you know."

In a comfortable small study with worn, soft chairs, stands a table and a typewriter. "I said I was a working girl," says Aracelis, "and this is my homework. Ever since I got my social service certificate, I have a job five days a week in my father's office as a typist. Sometimes I type out order forms for him at home."

"Aracelis is now the oldest in the family," says Señor Barrionuevo solemnly. "If I should die, she must be ready to take my place." Aracelis shrugs and smiles. Obviously, she does not take supporting the family or hard work too seriously.

Señor Barrionuevo, a patient, good-natured man, is manager of a wine distillery, and for her typist's work his daughter is paid an average of 600 *pesetas* a month or about fourteen dollars.

"I do not get an allowance as I know some American teen-agers do," explains Aracelis, "but I am allowed to keep my entire working salary for myself ... for books, records, movies, clothes or to save for vacations."

"Aracelis loves clothes," her mother said fondly. "For this summer alone, she has four new dresses—but they are 'grandmother gifts.' Otherwise, I think she would have had just one."

Clothes are almost a hobby with Aracelis, and she does most of her planning and buying for her wardrobe herself. Here in the south of Spain, few ready-made articles of apparel—except handbags, shoes, rain things and some beach clothing—are for sale in stores. Almost all dresses are made in homes, either by the women and girls for themselves or by neighborhood "modistas" who will run up a dress for as little as three dollars. Aracelis shops carefully for fabric, choosing either plain, strong colors or fine, subdued prints that can be accented with a bright belt or bow. Then she selects a picture from a fashion magazine or a pattern book—and her favorite dressmaker goes to work. "At La Asension we all wore convent uniforms," she explains, "and out of school we like to be butterflies."

Yet Aracelis is not a butterfly. At school, she was a serious student; at home, she is a combination baby-sitter, grandmother-companion and household helper. In the kitchen, there is a three-burner electric stove but the house has no other electric appliances except an iron and a radio. Laundry is done by hand in an open-air courtyard, just off the kitchen, and here, too, meat and fresh vegetables are kept in open-air shelves, screened off from flies. On a rush day, Aracelis can do the shopping in the town's market place or help out in the kitchen with gazpacho soup or paella, working with the three uniformed maids on an almost sisterly basis.

In her spare time, she loves to read, mostly historical novels or histories of the old Spanish kings and queens. Listening to the radio is a frequent pastime but Spain has no television, except two experimental stations in far-off Madrid and Barcelona. In fact, there are less than 500 TV sets in the whole country. And one afternoon a week, summer and winter, Aracelis works with a young people's Catholic Action group at her church, mending clothes or distributing food and medicine to the poor of Malaga. And there are many poor people in this sprawling old city of over 300,000 people.

In the town itself, there are sidewalk cafes, taxis, two air-conditioned theaters and big hotels with waiters in white gloves; but many of the crowded, small-street areas are impoverished and, immediately outside the town, the countryside becomes primitive, with simple, whitewashed cottages, black-garbed peasant women, donkeys carrying burdens along the main highways and great lumbering oxen pulling wagonloads of hand-cut sugar cane to the refinery. In this contrast of living, there are always *pobres* who need charitable help.

Religion plays a big part in the Barrioneuvo life. Aracelis' bedroom, on the second floor corner, overlooking the palm-shaded street, is shared with her fourteen-year-old sister. The narrow beds have attractive print spreads but a tiny, bare dressing table with a mirror and a big brown closet are the only other furnishings. The walls are not decked with pictures of popular singers or movie stars, in American teen-aged style; rather, Aracelis' "stars" are snapshots of her father and younger brother and one solemn picture of the Blessed Virgin and Christ Child in color.

Every Sunday, the family goes to Mass at the great brown stone cathedral, centuries old, which dominates the whole city of Malaga. And each night before dinner, Señor Barrionuevo leads his kneeling family and the maids in saying the prayers of the Rosary. This custom of family prayers is widely practiced in Spanish homes, and at about eight o'clock each evening the Rosary is broadcast over national radio. It becomes part of the background of life. Occasionally, in a busy home, a program of jazz music will be followed by the up-and-down singsong of the Rosary broadcast.

In Aracelis' clothes closet hang two sheer lace veils, one black and one white, and both mark important occasions in her teen-aged life: Mass and Semana Santa, and the bullfight. Semana Santa is, of course, the Holy Week ceremonies preceding Easter, which we have already mentioned.

The bullfight season is purely social, that exciting time from Easter Day until late October, when the great beige-stone bullring in Malaga comes alive with noise and color. Bullfights are then held every Sunday afternoon and on holidays—and every day during one week in August, when Malaga has its annual fair. Although soccer is popular, it is still the bullfighters who are the glamour boys of the country and whose posters plaster every lamp-post and country wall in Spain. Once last season, Aracelis was chosen with five other pretty teen-agers to sit in the President's box at the bullfight, a place of honor. She was chosen for a number of reasons: she is pretty, her father is a prominent businessman, and she comes from a good family and is therefore "social." The last reason is probably the most important in society-conscious Spain. On this gay occasion, the white veil was worn over a high comb, flowing down over a modified gypsy dress—red and white dotted percale with a short, ruffled skirt, which Aracelis designed herself. In Andalusian fashion, her dark hair was pinned at one side with a rose.

"It was one of the most exciting days of my life," she said, as she modeled the clothes for us. "I love the bullfight and see at least five or six every year."

The hot Spanish sun is beginning to sink toward the sea and a fresh breeze strikes up from the water. It is early evening but, instead of drawing to a close, the second half of the Spanish day is just beginning. Life here seems to be lived with a special clock.

"This is the time of day," says Aracelis, "when the 'powdered milks' like to dance or go to a movie. (The first movie starts at six, the last at eleven.) We never go out on separate dates—of course—and we never go out after dinner. So I guess we're always home by ten o'clock, at the latest."

Up to a point, it would be easy for any average American teen-ager to join Aracelis and the other 'powdered milks' in their life in Malaga. These young people like to sing and dance to the old flamenco songs, but they also love rock and roll. They like Spanish-made movies but they also are fans of Tony Curtis, Burt Lancaster and Gregory Peck. They like beach picnics and swimming together, even though always in groups or sternly chaperoned. American teen-agers would find their Spanish counterparts both older and younger in their ways than they are themselves.

Aracelis will tell you, for instance, that she has no special boy friend "but I expect to be married when I am nineteen, just three years from now. It must be someone my parents approve of—and I'd like him to be an engineer or a doctor. And I must always live in Malaga. How could anyone live away from this blue sea and wonderful sun?"

Thus, while the average American teen-aged girl

will be busy as a secretary, a student nurse or a salesgirl or while she is just planning her courses for a second or third year of college, Aracelis will already be a young matron, tending a home of her own and probably singing flamenco lullabies. And many other wealthy, privileged Spanish teen-agers are just like Aracelis in "profile": pretty, well-trained, contented home girls. And home is exactly where they want to be.

«««««« »»»»»»»

Luis Hernandez also lives in Malaga and he, too, is just sixteen. In his part of town, the old streets twist and bend until the tiny, overhanging balconies, burdened with flowerpots, seem to touch in mid-air. It is noisy and crowded, filled with people in every daylight hour and even until late at night. Rickety candy stands, bright with cellophane and cheap plastic toys, lean against the curbs. In the doorways, old women in faded, well-patched black sit sewing and chatting, and dozens of cats sun themselves along the window sills. The movement, the crowds and the children playing and shouting over the rough cobblestones give the neighborhood a bustling, carnival air every day of the week. Luis' home is One Huerto de Monjaz, a poor street in a back section of town, apartment number ten, three flights up and the last door on the left.

Through an inside, open-air courtyard, painted a bright, chalky blue and climbing with geraniums, up two flights of blue stairs, scrubbed clean but still smelling of cats, along a narrow passageway open to the courtyard and to the sky and into the back of the building. This is Luis' home.

This five-room apartment for five people, with water and light included, rents at only four dollars and forty cents a month. But the rooms are so small that a sewing machine, covered with a brightly embroidered cloth, and four straight, cane-seated chairs crowd the front parlor. And I noticed that, in the tiny dining room, Luis' aunt, who has cared for the family since his mother died six years ago, had to crowd and push to pass between the single china cabinet and the square, heavy table that sits in the middle of the room. There was no other furniture.

But this home, a typical apartment for a Spanish workingman, is unimportant to Luis. Here he is restless, impatient and often bad-tempered. His aunt putters about the house, sewing and cleaning, in a blue and white dotted dress so old and threadbare that the white dots are falling out. With her—and with his strict father—he is well-mannered and quiet. But with his brother and sisters he is different. The older sister is married and lives away from home but his younger sister, a handsome, dark-haired girl of twenty-eight, is still at home and with her he bickers constantly, calling her bitterly "my terrible stepmother." To his only brother, a lanky twenty-one-year-old with whom he shares a bedroom, he barely speaks. "My brother is interested in nothing but his girl friend," Luis says. "We have nothing to talk about."

For most of his life, shyness and lack of money kept Luis locked in the narrow, crowded streets around his home. Until six months ago he had never been outside the city limits. Then, one rainy winter day, he took a twelve-cent bus ride—crowded in with shoppers, tourists and ragged native gypsies with baskets of plastic combs and fans to sell—to the fishing village of Torremolinos, seven miles away. One short trip in sixteen years—and yet Luis firmly believes that by the time he is twenty-one, he will have made a voyage to New York.

Except for his outsized dreams, Luis is much like other working class boys his age in Malaga. While he was from six to ten years old, he went to a school taught by Catholic nuns, learned his catechism, to read and write a little, some arithmetic and some history. At ten, he was ready for work. (In Spain, it is required by law that every child go to school until he is ten years old, but there are so many more children than schools that many boys and girls—no matter how eager—never get inside a schoolhouse).

If Luis had been a wealthy young Spaniard, or had an outstanding I.Q., he might have gone on to a private secondary school with his tuition paid for by parents or a special scholarship fund provided by the state for very bright students. If he had been interested in crafts, mechanics or electronics, he might have applied (and then patiently waited his turn) to get into one of the good State-run trade schools in Malaga; or, he might have hired out immediately as an "apprentice" at about twenty cents a day, working and studying for from three to six years until he could qualify as an assistant or *maestro* in such trades as carpentry, shoemaking, plumbing or metal working. (Luis's father is a *maestro* mechanic, earning twenty dollars a week, and his brother is an apprentice in the same factory, earning four dollars and fifty cents).

But Luis chose to try earning his living at just ten years old, and without special training. Luckily, he has a talent. He can draw. "My big career started with Marilyn Monroe," he explains with a laugh. "But I knew I could draw when I was only four years old." Then he liked to draw with chalk on the rough cobblestones in front of his apartment building. Sometimes passers-by would pause to look and toss him a *peseta* or two for his work. At thirteen, he began studying art at night school but gave it up almost at once.

"I don't like to be told what to do," he said rebelliously. But a commercial artist saw some of Luis' art school sketches and hired him to tint photographs at the equivalent of seventy-five cents a picture. Luis never went to school again. Instead, he worked three hours a day—and then spent the money for food and to sit through two or three movies every afternoon and evening.

"The soft music in the movies is what I liked best," Luis explained. "I could think and feel away from everything. I didn't even tell my family where I went."

One day after a movie, he bought a postcard picture of Marilyn Monroe. Later, he copied the picture in black and white, enlarging it about ten times, but keeping it accurate in every detail. A neighborhood friend put the picture in her dressmaking shop—and a wealthy customer saw it. She asked him to sketch portraits of her children. Other customers followed and now Luis sometimes earns as much as twenty-five dollars a week—more than his father, more than most teachers and policemen, in fact, more than most grown men in Spain, except politicians, professional men and very wealthy industrialists and landowners.

But although his family is proud of him, his brother and sisters are jealous, and his money has only made trouble at home for Luis. His brother said harshly, "You are only a good drawer, you will never be an artist."

Maria, fiercely hot-tempered, yet possessive, said, "We do not even know where he keeps his money! I tell him to stay humble and to learn another trade but he has a big head. He won't even buy us a radio."

Luis, easily hurt and almost too shy to talk back, answered sullenly, "I pay five dollars a week for my board here. I am saving my money to go to art school in Madrid. And who wants a radio? It would cost sixty dollars and the house would be full of nothing but noise."

In his discontent with his own life, Luis has come to love what he thinks is "American life," most of which he has picked up from movies. Though musicals and gangster movies are his favorites, he still firmly believes he has an accurate picture of the United States.

"I like the Americans for their freedom and independence. There is work and money for everyone. Every man is an individual. Everyone does what he likes."

Luis even tries to dress like an American teen-ager. He usually wears moccasins, white T-shirts and well-pegged blue levis for which he pays three dollars a pair. Through the movies, too, he has some strong ideas about American juvenile delinquency and cannot understand it at all. "Why should anyone do such things—wrecking schools and stealing cars—in a country with so much work and money? Here a boy might steal if he was hungry or a gypsy might take a bicycle or something out of a garden. But no one from a good family would make trouble just for trouble."

Even though he has never been in "trouble" of any kind, Luis is carefully watched at home; he never smokes, sometimes drinks a bottle of beer on Sundays but never the local wine, both good and cheap. He has never driven a car and is usually in the apartment around midnight, at the latest. Recently, he stayed out with a group of boys until half-past twelve and his father told him that a second such mistake would mean no visits to the beach for a week.

But most often, during the day at least, Luis' life is independent. Usually, he lies in bed until ten, getting up only when the apartment is quiet and his aunt is out at the street market. Then he breakfasts on bread and marmalade and cold milk. When he is not doing portraits, he may go to the beach, wander around the city streets with a boy friend and, once in a while, go to the town museum or the public library to read humor magazines.

Two nights a week and most Saturday afternoons, Luis spends with his girl friend, a pretty sixteen-year-old named Maria Carmen. Luis blushes fiercely when he talks about her, partly because she is his first girl friend and partly because "love" is taken so seriously in Spain.

"She is not bold but very chaste," he began carefully. "I met her one night at a dance in a private house. We just danced in the courtyard. Maria Carmen came with her brother and he introduced us. Sometimes we go for walks together, sometimes to a movie—usually her brother is with us. But she is a *friend*," he insists, "not my *novia*."

Unlike most Spaniards his age, Luis dislikes the bullfight intensely. "I don't like crowds," he explains. "I don't like the noise and the push. And I don't like to see animals killed. I used to go when I was younger but have other interests now."

Against another of Spain's great traditions, Luis is also a rebel. He has decided he no longer wants to go to church. His old aunt, an ardent churchgoer herself, simply shrugs. "Young people get such ideas but they come around," she says.

"I can explain myself," Luis began (with religion,

as with so many things, he is almost too shy to express himself). "I am a Catholic and I believe in God, but I don't go to church and I don't believe in priests. All my friends are indifferent, too. When we were little, everyone made such a fuss about it. The day I made my First Communion, I wore a white suit and was paraded through the streets and everyone acted like I was a saint. Now I am awfully skeptical." (Luis was, of course, speaking only for the limited number of boys and girls with whom he was associated. The majority of young people in Malaga adhere closely to their belief in the Catholic faith).

Politically, Luis is extra-young for his teen years. He knows nothing, for instance, of the giant air bases in Spain, manned by Americans and costing over $300,000,000, that cast the shadows of military jet planes over his country. And he knows just as little about the workings of his own government, except for the existence of its Head, Generalissimo Franco. He is interested in freedom, but only in freedom in his own life—freedom from the boredom of a small flat and a family he feels does not understand him in the least.

When he is twenty-one, Luis Hernandez, like all young Spanish men, will have to serve in the army for eighteen months to two years. "I'll be glad to go," he said with conviction. "The army tries to send boys as far away from their home towns as they can. Maybe it will give me a chance to see something besides these same streets. I would like to see and do new things. I just don't want *old* things any more. I don't like old streets, old churches, the old way of living. I like my country but I want a new kind of life, I want to be *myself*."

Although he is so quick to criticize his present life, Luis—like many young Spaniards—does not want the responsibility of figuring out how to change it. Perhaps to earn a living or get an education in a poor country is problem enough: perhaps the young Spaniards do not want added responsibilities.

Luis smiled and seemed almost relieved when I closed my notebook, relieved that this "thinking" about himself and his life was over. "I have no real dream," he said. "I will work, learn to speak English—and then what? Time will tell me what to do."

«««««««« »»»»»»»»

Two young people, same nationality, same age, same town. I wondered if they knew each other. Aracelis Barrionuevo-Bolin answered my question graciously and with a light smile. "Luis Hernandez who lives on Huerto de Monjaz? No, I do not know him. I am afraid he is not one of the 'powdered milks.' "

Luis' answer was more abrupt and bitter. "Of course I don't know her. Who would ever introduce *me* to a girl from the good section of town?"

Chapter VII

BRAVO! THE BULLS!

THE BULLFIGHT (as everyone must know by now who can read or watch movies and television) is the national spectacle of Spain. But to speak of bull *fights* or bull *fighting* to a Spaniard would only confuse him. He doesn't regard the *corrida* ("the running of the bull") as a *fight* in any sense of the word. In the first place, there can be only one winner and there is no doubt about the outcome—the bull has been bred and raised to die in the *plaza de toros*. True, he might wound or even kill the matador assigned to destroy him, but in this event, another matador will step in and finish the job. There is one exception to this—the rarely invoked custom of *indulto*. This means that, if a bull has demonstrated enormous and furious valor in his attacks against horses and *toreros*, the spectators may appeal to the Authority (those officials and judges sitting in a special box) to spare his life. This is usually done by wild applause or the waving of handkerchiefs all over the plaza. Should the appeal of the public be granted, the bull will be led out of the ring alive, but, since he has probably been wounded gravely by this time, he will be mercifully shot and killed in the corrals behind the bull ring. So even the rare *indulto* only adds a few extra moments to the bull's life.

It is this fact—that the bull cannot "win"—which makes the art of bullfighting unattractive to many visitors to Spain. They believe, and correctly, that the bull has no chance of getting out of the ring alive, and this seems to them to make the whole proposition cruel and unsporting. Further, they realize, and again correctly, that the bull doesn't *want* to be in the ring in the first place and, in many fights, will leap the barriers to make a futile flight for freedom.

All in all, bullfighting frequently appears—to the non-Spanish eye—as a savage game in which men are rewarded for torturing and killing a dumb animal who, if given a voice in the matter, would infinitely prefer to spend his life grazing in peaceful pastures and keeping well clear of all encounters with "civilized" man.

However, despite these objections from foreigners, Spaniards love the bullfight and it remains one of the most prominent spectacles in Spain. In recent years, it has received some competition from professional football (soccer to us and *futbol* to the Spaniards) but nevertheless the bull rings of Spain are still jammed every sunny Sunday by thousands and thousands of *aficionados* or "fans." Most Spaniards even allow their children to witness the *corridas*. It is a common sight to see a whole family sitting in a row, splendid in starched Sunday best, nibbling sweet cakes and nuts and cheering on the bulls.

The bullfight season runs roughly from Easter through October, and in the large cities of Madrid, Barcelona, Malaga and so forth there will be an important *corrida* every week. In addition, many of the villages have their own rings, frequently the most imposing building in town except the church, and fights will be staged there whenever an impresario can attract a card of matadors with sufficient reputation to bring in a full house. Also, larger cities stage week-long festivals every year—usually commemorating the city's patron saint—during which there will be bullfights every afternoon, processions every evening and unorganized merrymaking all through the night. The country towns usually confine their celebrations to one weekend, one bullfight —and whatever other spontaneous gaiety happens to spring up.

<<<<<<<<< >>>>>>>>>

It is difficult to explain why bullfighting had such an important and respected place in Spanish culture, and in the lives of Spanish men and women through the centuries. It is frequently inferred that Spaniards must be inherently cruel to tolerate such a barbarous national pastime, but this attempt at a national or ethnical explanation simply is not valid. The British are not similarly condemned for their fox hunting; some Americans savor cockfighting (it is legal in three states, practiced illegally in many others) and hunting with a gun is a favorite sport with millions of Americans. Our televised prize fights, high in popularity in the United States, would strike many people of the world as horrible barbarism. Yet British and American sports are seldom "explained" as showing a cruel streak of national length and proportion.

Also, popular as it is there, bullfighting did not begin in Spain nor is it confined to that country. According to most authorities, the "sport" began in Rome. And today it is practiced throughout Mexico, South America, Portugal and in parts of France—in France, however, it is officially illegal, but it is tolerated in the south. Most top Spanish matadors pick up extra cash by springtime fighting in and around the town of Arles, in the south of France, much as American baseball players add to their off-season income by exhibitions or games in Cuba or Japan.

But if bullfighting didn't originate in Spain, it is there that it was organized over the centuries into a complex and ritualistic spectacle. The first "bullfights" undoubtedly occurred on the plains of Spain, a few thousand years ago, with wild bulls and equally wild young men battling it out against the horns with spear, rock, clubs or anything else that came readily to hand. Eventually and inevitably, however, refinements took place. As time passed, the man mounted a horse and killed his bull with lance thrusts, and this gave the sport a social tone since well-bred horses were man's first Cadillacs, and the men who owned them were naturally to be found among the aristocrats. Later, it became a custom to dispatch the bull with the man on foot and only after suitable cape flourishes. This laid the groundwork and ground rules for the *corrida* as it is still displayed today in Spain. The man on the ground facing the bull became more and more important; the horsemen were relegated to positions of secondary significance, and the greatest honors went to those men on foot who dared to work closely with the savage bulls, diverting their attacks with formal and elegant cape passes and finally dispatching them with a sword thrust.

<<<<<<<<< >>>>>>>>>

The present fighting bull of Spain is a pure descendent of the wild Toro Bravo who roamed the Iberian peninsula thousands of years ago. He has little in common with *our* farm bull, the full and heavy domestic animal whose moments of glory are usually confined to running an occasional farmer up a tree or butting his head irritably against the side of a Ford pickup truck. Today's *toro bravo* of Spain will weigh a sleek and functional thousand pounds or more, he can outrun a race horse in short charges and his horns have been bred into powerful, needle-sharp weapons. His weight is forward, centering in the great crest of lifting muscles above his shoulders, the muscles which can drive his horns through inch-thick planks and hoist a kicking horse and scrambling rider four feet off the ground. The horses used in today's bull ring by the picadors are heavily padded, incidentally. They may suffer from fright or a tumble, but they are protected against goring.

We once visited a bull-raising ranch near Cadiz. The pasturage was lush and rolling, cut through with running streams, all far from distracting city noises. The Spaniards who work at these *ganaderías* or bull farms lead a lonely life, like sailors or lighthouse keepers. During the day, they ride the vast pastures at a safe and sensible distance from the bull herds, making sure their charges are in good health and temper. They keep out of range of the bulls' weak eyesight as much as possible and for two reasons: one, a common-sense precaution against a whimsical goring, and two, because the convention of the bullfight requires that the bulls have as little sight or knowledge of horses and men as possible before encountering them in the great arenas. Bulls learn very quickly and a bull that had "pasture practice" in charging would be doubly dangerous to the matador in the bullring.

At night, the ranch workers gather in their shacks near the horse barns. Here they cook their own food, usually a heavy soup or a beef and chicken paella with saffron rice, and drink wine around the fire. The darkness closes in about them, and occasionally someone will produce a guitar and play the music of gypsies, which permeates all Spain. Most of these farm workers have never seen a bullfight. This would, after all, require money for a bus trip, a hotel room and a ticket to the arena, and these ranch workers are poorly paid. But those who can read watch the newspapers carefully for news of their "babies" and how they met their fates in the arenas throughout Spain.

Each bull in the herd is familiar to them; they watch this or that little black one with the stubby horns mature over the years into an animal of awesome size and strength. They notice his speed, observe him clear a boulder like a hunter or charge blindly over the meadow when stung by a wasp or from the sheer exuberance of his growing muscles and fighting spirit. When the bull leaves for Salamanca or Granada or Madrid, the ranch workers wait confidently for the report of his fight. On the huge posters announcing every *corrida,* the bulls are given billing—"from the ranch of Don Jose So-and-So"—and each bull enters the ring with the colored ribbons of his ranch flying from the muscle hump behind the horns. Hence, each bull represents the skill, care and concern of the workers back home. If the bull is given an ovation for strength and bravery after it has been killed, the ranch owner or his representative is asked to circle the ring with the matador while the crowd applauds. When these glorious things happen, the lonely men around the bunkhouse fire read the newspaper accounts to each other and beam as proudly as parents whose son has scored the winning touchdown for his school.

<<<<<<<<< >>>>>>>>>

During the season when the young bulls are tested —these rituals are called *tientas*—the bull ranches explode with carnival gaiety. The week of testing is one long *fiesta,* with business and pleasure mixing in happy proportions. These parties are private, of course, but, with luck, the passing tourist may be invited to join the fun. There is no prescription for such good fortune; it will strike with all probability from the most unlikely and unexpected source. The elderly and reserved Spanish couple whose table adjoins yours at a sidewalk cafe may assist you in understanding the menu and ordering breakfast. Perhaps you'll get to chatting. You've already seen such and such, been to this place or that, and they will urge you not to miss the altar paintings in the old church in the next village or to stop at the *parador* (government-run hotel) high in the next ridge of mountains. Spaniards are understandably proud of their country and usually pleased by the attention and approval of tourists. Thus small friendships spring up easily.

At any rate, to return to our fictional Spanish couple who helped to order your fresh melon, toast and eggs. It may be that their brother owns a bull ranch or is a bullfight impresario or works in some capacity or other with persons who do own ranches and stage bullfights. They may suggest then that a *tienta* is most interesting to observe and to arrange your participation in this would be their pleasure.

Our introduction to a *tienta* came in just this unlikely manner. On an early trip to Spain, we were staying at a beach hotel on the island of Ibiza, and at an adjoining table was a cheerful and typical Spanish family, a confident and adoring father, a quiet and watchful mother and three chubby, elaborately groomed but rather plain teen-aged daughters. Papa kept his wife and daughters giggling throughout the meals with jokes and stories and it was impossible for us not to share in their good humor, at least with smiles at their smiles, and a good, warm feeling over their obvious pleasure in their own company. However, the girls were trying to diet and Papa was comically outraged by their preference for fruits and salads as opposed to his own ferocious delight in all six courses, from mixed fried fish to white cheese. He teased the girls about their concern with weight and pointed out *los Americanos* who were both slim *and* on their fourth course.

After a day or so, we were all good friends, talking from table to table. Soon we had our coffee together in the evenings and one night Papa said, "You should know *more* about the bullfight. Now a *tienta* is a most interesting phase to see and my brother goes each spring to the ranch of Don So-and-So for these affairs. If you would like me to arrange something —" We *would,* and kindly Papa *did* make all arrangements. The subject of diet had made us good friends.

<<<<<<<<<< >>>>>>>>>>

Each bull ranch has its own small bull ring and it is here that the young bulls are tested, to see whether or not they have the calibre to appear in major *corridas*. Mounted men with blunt pics test each bull's courage and will to fight. If the bull reacts bravely to punishment and continues to attack the horse, it will be judged "brave" and will be sent back out to the range, to mature into a fighting bull. If he shows timidity or excess nervousness, he is consigned to the beef herd and one may encounter him next on a platter in some good restaurant in Madrid or Barcelona.

The owner of the ranch and his foreman sit high in the arena and make the judgments on each bull. The guests of the ranch owner fill the remaining seats to watch the show. After each day's "testing," young cows, or rejected young bulls, are turned loose in the ring for anyone who wants to try his skill with a fighting cape. There is a large group of *aficionados practicantes* in Spain (that is, fans who play with the young cows and bulls in amateur fights, besides watching the full *corridas*) and these men often put on a good and frequently very funny show. These special *aficionados* come from all classes and are united only by the wistful thought that they would rather be *matadores de toros* than doctors, lawyers, merchants or butcher boys. A furious young cow is a pretty tricky animal to handle with only a cape, and more often than not at the *tientas* a paunchy, perspiring performer (most likely a dignified businessman fifty-one weeks of the year) finds himself rolling in the dust while the audience is rolling in the aisles with laughter. But it is often at these *tientas,* too, that local farm boys or fledgling *toreros* get the first tastes of triumph from handling a cow with skill and courage, spurred on by *"oles"* and applause.

Frequently, full-fledged matadors are on hand, as guests of the ranch, and their presence adds glamor and excitement to the *tienta*. As a professional singer or dancer may be called on to entertain friends at a private party, so the matador will go through a series of passes in the ranch bullring. He does not wear his splendid, glittering *traje de luces* for this type of appearance but a *traje corto*, a short jacket of black, a broad-brimmed Andalusian hat and tight trousers tucked into short boots. He will be quite serious about his work and make every effort to do a good job—for who knows what new contracts may result from an impressive show before the right people?

At night, the ranch-owner will entertain his guests in his home with dinner, wines and bullfight talk until late into the night. Inevitably, a troupe of gypsies will have been hired to sing and dance flamenco on the terrace under the stars. The *tienta* is a time when two important things must be proven: the courage of the young bulls and the hospitality of the ranch owner who, in Spanish tradition, must lavish attention on his guests.

<<<<<<<<<< >>>>>>>>>>

In Spain, there are "little" *corridas* and "big" *corridas*, and one particular small *corrida* sticks in my memory because the star of the afternoon was the same young man who ordinarily sold us our veal cutlets and spiced sausage in the village meat market. He was the butcher's son, about eighteen years old, slim, blond and very wild. The village had nicknamed him "The Young Earthquake," partly because of his daring in amateur bullfights and partly because he drove through the narrow, cobbled streets on a motorcycle at too-many miles an hour. The Earthquake was asked to fight a very young bull at a charity bullfight staged in our village on Christmas Day. For weeks before, the village was plastered with posters announcing the *corrida*, lovingly hand-painted by The Earthquake's relatives. A makeshift bullring of weathered planks was erected in a sandy field outside town. The Earthquake prepared himself for the *corrida* by practicing passes with a cape in the butcher shop—with his apron—and by using "sword thrusts" to butcher cows (to be sold in the shop, of course) in his father's slaughterhouse at one edge of the village. Precisely at five o'clock on this windy, cold Christmas Day, the villagers settled on wobbly plank tiers, someone wound a portable victrola and the exciting music of the bullfight sounded out into the afternoon. Standing by, in case of real trouble, was a professional bullfighter from a nearby city. But nothing could be done to save The Earthquake from a near-disastrous afternoon. The bull was small, with horns no bigger than bananas, but he was strong and full of bounce. The Earthquake, blond hair slicked back, face pale, was a paragon of courage but totally without skill or common sense. Every time he unfurled his red cape, planted his feet firmly in the ground and shouted an insulting *"vaca!"* (cow!) at the young bull, the animal simply charged him, butted him soundly or tossed him in the air. Before long, both "matador" and "bull" were charging around the ring, looking like nothing more serious than two muddy little boys caught in a furious wrestling match. The spectators applauded wildly because it was, after all, Christmas Day.

The following morning, I saw The Earthquake in his father's shop, waiting on customers and solemnly accepting congratulations on his fight. An eye was black, a cheek patched in three places and he moved with noticeable stiffness. A rumor spread through the village that the townspeople were going to take up a collection to send him to Madrid to become a full-fledged *torero*. It was civic duty; this was a man of great courage, he would bring honor to the entire village. But as The Earthquake's bruises faded, so did the talk. Some time later, the word spread that he had given up bullfighting forever. He was a fighter of too-great heart; he had decided his courage would kill his own mother with worry. As far as I know, The Earthquake never entered a bullring again.

«««««« »»»»»»

There is an old and very gay Spanish song that ends its chorus refrain with the words ". . . *and the seventh of July, San Fermin!*" That is the starting date of the annual bullfight *fiesta* at Pamplona, a week made famous even in America by Ernest Hemingway's *The Sun Also Rises*.

This is the *fiesta* which venerates Saint Fermin— and all the bulls and all the bullfighters in all of

Spain. Crowds from every corner of Spain and all Europe jam the northern city of Pamplona for the event and most major hotels have their rooms booked a year in advance. We found a room in a private apartment—the children had been boarded out with grandmother for the week, father slept in his office and the *señora* of the house put up a cot in the kitchen for herself. The revenue she obtained each year for renting three bedrooms to tourists for San Fermin was enough to give the entire family a country vacation during the month of August.

What happens during the great *fiesta* of San Fermin? Bullfights are staged every afternoon, with the greatest names in bullfighting vying with each other for the season's honors. There are daily parades of the curious San Fermin figures, papier-mâché structures two stories high, with great, painted heads and gaudy floating costumes, all propelled by men underneath who waltz through the streets, preceded by little bands and groups of singers. It was a strange and exciting feeling to be awakened early one morning by high, lilting music and to see a pair of staring, painted eyes bobbing just above the level of the apartment window sill!

San Fermin is traditionally a time of "good fellowship," and many of the young male Spaniards try to celebrate for all seven days without going to bed. A nap may be snatched at a cafe table or open doorway but never, never in one's own bed. The streets are crowded and full of noise around the clock. At six in the morning and at six at night—

any time—groups gather together in cafes or street corners to sing. And everyone wears a triangular silk scarf of red, knotted around the neck. Singing and dancing in the open makes the whole town look like a bouncing, ducking, twirling mass of animated sound.

Certainly the Spaniards (and their visitors) seemed to be drinking wine constantly during the fiesta week but so deeply is the idea of "good fellowship" imbedded that there is no bad temper, no disorder and no rowdiness. Everyone is a friend of everybody else. To give a personal example of this, we ate dinner one late, loud evening in a simple, second-floor cafe on the main square. The restaurant was crowded and diners took turns singing songs particular to their part of Spain. It was so exciting that we stayed too long and spent too much money—in fact, our bill was several dollars (in *pesetas*) more than we had in our pockets. We explained this to the waiter and asked if we might come back in the morning to square the debt. A solemn little man at the next table jumped up and insisted on paying our bill. Where, we asked, could we possibly find him to repay his money—and his kindness? *Repay him,* he asked in surprise. *It was his pleasure to treat us.* Did we not realize this was *San Fermin?* Such is the spirit that fills the town for a full, noisy week.

Second to the splendid *corridas,* the highpoint of the festivities is the actual "running of the bulls" through the crooked old streets of the town. In this part of Spain, a man is not a man until he has "run before the bulls." Certain streets, leading from a bullpen ring into the arena of the *plaza de toros,* are barricaded chin-high with heavy lumber. Once inside the barriers, there is no escape except to vault the high sides. The young men of the town—or any man with courage—crowd inside the barriers, some close to the bullpen gate, others straggling on and on down the blocks to the *plaza de toros,* in varying degrees of foolhardiness and courage. At six o'clock in the morning, for all seven days of the *fiesta,* the town hall clock strikes the hour, then a distant gunshot signal sounds in the still morning air—and the bullpen door is opened. First comes a tinny sound of bells, announcing the lumbering belled oxen who start the bulls on their journey through the streets. Then an ominous heavy trample as the bulls start running. Then a murmur and a rush as the young men begin to move. And, finally, a roar of the whole crowd, inside and outside the barriers, as the tumult of men and animals rush toward the bullring and safety.

Most of the "runners" manage to reach the bullring before the bulls, others plaster themselves against the barriers in fright and let the pounding herd go by (usually six bulls and two oxen), while many stumble and fall, then try to roll out of the way of the sharp hoofs and hooking horns. In some years, runners have been fatally gored; other times there have been minor casualties. But always there are cuts, scratches and innumerable bumps and bruises. After he has "run before the bulls," a man may have the honor of wearing his red San Fermin kerchief in reverse, with the knot behind and the red triangle under the throat. By seven in the morning, every sidewalk cafe is filled with excited runners, kerchiefs reversed, eating ham and drinking black coffee while they boast about their bravery and the nearness of the bulls.

The first morning I watched the running of the bulls, there was a misting rain and the sky was dark, even for early morning. The streets were both noisy and silent, with the air of a crowd at a picnic apprehensive about a violent storm. I stood on a box to look just over the barrier and down at the little cobbled street. The melancholy bells and the distant gun-shot were like sounds of terror. Moments later, the bulls passed before me with frightening speed, but close enough to give off an animal odor of hide, hair and dampness and to let us hear their short, angry breath as they ran. Traditionally, women are not allowed to run before the bulls. And I, for one, was delighted not to have to make any greater show of courage than crouching behind the fence. Why, then, do so many young men—through the centuries—choose to risk death to run before the bulls? Because that *is traditional;* a true man must show courage, especially at San Fermin.

«««««« »»»»»»»

And now for the bullfight, not necessarily at Pamplona, but in any big city in Spain. The first thing one notices is the pulse of excitement in the arena, the tension gripping the thousands of spectators. Seats in the shade are expensive but there the chances of sunstroke are considerably less and the matadors tend to work in front of the high-priced seats. It is possible to rent a thin, hard pillow for a couple of pesetas which, hard as it is, is infinitely preferable to the concrete benches which circle the arena in unbroken lines. The designers of Spanish bullrings seem to have a flattering notion of the graceful posteriors of human animals for the space allotted each seat is just about wide enough to accommodate a small, diet-conscious, five-year-old child. But the crowding and confusion is all part of the atmosphere. The mood is carnival but tense. The music blares from a brass band. Hawkers peddle soft drinks, gum, peanuts and little cakes. Everyone chatters and stares about. The president's box (where the judges and officials sit) is decked with banners, colorful shawls and flowers. At the *fiesta corridas,* the Spanish ladies will likely wear their shawls, high combs and lace mantillas and at any *corrida,* their well-groomed heads will be decked with roses or twists of jasmine.

There is an old saying in Spain that the bullfight is the only thing in the country that starts on time. Unlike lots of old sayings, this one is thoroughly true. Anyone who comes late will miss the most colorful phase of the *corrida.*

At the appointed hour, there is a thrilling drumbeat, then a trumpet sounds ominously in descending thirds. A great gate swings open and the

Bravo! The Bulls! · 123

bullfighters make their entrance, walking in slow, pigeon-toed steps across the hot sand, followed by their assistants—banderilleros, picadores and punterilleros—walking in three stately columns of medieval color and pageantry. Each afternoon's program features three matadors and their companies—and six bulls. The crowd stands and roars an ovation.

The matadors salute the presiding official and retire behind a wooden barrier which keeps the bull from making a too-close inspection of the thousands who have paid their pesetas to see him killed.

The matadors test the wind with their capes, occasionally dampening the trailing edge with water and even dragging it a bit in the dust, to pick up weight and give them a more certain control of its swing.

Then a hush settles. The trumpets sound again. The *toril* gate (the gate from the bullpen) is opened and the bull charges out into the brilliant sun, looking, in Ernest Hemingway's phrase, "for something to kill."

The bullfight is phased in three acts: horses, banderillas and sword. The picadors, in act one, are usually mounted on weary, bag-of-bones horses whose vocal cords have been severed to prevent them from making any noise and who wear a black sash over the eye that will be facing the bull. The bull is incited to charge the horse from the side, while the mounted picador jabs *el toro* with a long, strong and sharply pic-ed lance. The pica-ing of the bull is meant to weaken its shoulder muscles and bring its horns down to a more manageable height. The matador has to kill reaching over those horns and, *aficionados* point out, if there were no pica-ing, there would be very few matadors alive in Spain today.

Next the *banderillas* are placed, sometimes by the matador himself, more often by an assistant. The *banderillas* are short sticks, twisted with colored paper and ending with sharp, steel barbs. These are placed two at a time, by a man who runs toward the bull, diverts himself sideways and plunges the barbs sharply in the bull's muscle hump, above the shoulders. From the spectator standpoint, this is usually one of the highpoints of the *corrida*, since the man-and-bull drama is solitary, rapid and precise and the tiny glittering figure of the man has all the quick, formal grace of a ballet.

And finally, after two of the *toreros* have "played" the bull with large magenta and yellow capes, in order to let the third matador study his habits and movements, that matador takes over his bull completely. He is alone in the great arena with nothing more than his courage and a small red flannel cape to prepare the bull for the most important act of this spectacle, the somewhat oddly described "moment of truth."

After playing the bull through a series of passes, the matador is expected—ideally—to kill the bull with a single sword thrust between the horns, severing the spinal cord in one merciful stroke. If the kill is good and clean, the matador will be awarded an ear from the dead bull as a token of his skill. If the bullfight has been very good, he will get two ears, and, in certain rare cases, a tail and a hoof. With these trophies in hand, he then makes a circuit of the ring, acknowledging the applause and stopping to collect gifts and tokens thrown to him by the audience. These may include goatskins of wine (and tradition demands that he take a long, manly swig from several of these), bunches of flowers and even such personal items as slippers, compacts, hats, purses and hair ribbons. All of these last are collected by assistants and thrown back into the audience, where they are passed from hand to hand until they reach their original owners.

In reverse, when a matador lacks skill or courage or when his ineptitude subjects the bull to a too-prolonged ordeal, he is rewarded with hoots and jeers and even with those hard, little cushions hurled out onto the sand. The emotional Spaniards take their bullfights seriously and are either generous or extremely harsh as judges of performance.

That, in brief, is a bullfight. If it is an unskilled one, you may be repelled by it. As you file out with the hot, exhausted crowd, you may ask what keeps this strange spectacle alive through the centuries. But if it is a good *corrida*—a very good one—you won't have to ask. You may not approve, you may decide never to go again but you *will* have an understanding of the bullfight. For on a sunny day in Spain, you will have bought a ticket to see an act of courage, colorful and traditional, and whether courage is pointless or not, it is always worth looking at.

Chapter VIII

SNAPSHOTS IN SPAIN

Any travel map is pinpointed with little "memory flags" and usually each flag stands for a person. Museums are important, scenery is important—but it is people that make the warmest memories and are the best and mose rewarding index to a country itself.

For instance, the great Cathedral in Toledo may be something to cherish in memory forever, but chances are it will be sharpened and highlighted by the guide one talked with, or the little old lady who lent a handkerchief to cover the head or a postcard salesman in a nearby cafe who pulled out pictures of his children. *There* is the beauty of travel: the opportunity to collect a private album of people and memories. Here are some verbal snapshots from my special collection—Spaniards whose pictures do not fade.

«««««« »»»»»»»

Anna Rodriguez: Anna worked in a tiny tobacco shop that also sold stamps and camera film. She was in her late twenties, but looked fifty, pale and fat and gloomy. Anna always wore black because her father had died some years before; now she sighed against life in general and the effort of pushing a stamp or cigarette across the counter. Her home was one room behind the shop; her counter, where she sat nine hours a day, was decked with four potted geraniums, a sleepy white cat and a small statue of the Blessed Virgin. Anna even ate her breakfast at this counter, pausing grumpily to sell cigarettes to early risers or fishermen back from the morning stint at the beach. Sometimes, she supped a bowl of weak coffee, floating with bread; on other mornings, she ate cold scraps from the night before, fried fish or vegetables, made palatable with a squeeze of fresh lemon juice. To anyone who listened, she complained of indigestion, insomnia and assorted maladies, shifting uneasily on her hard wooden chair. A terrible thing had happened to Anna, bit by bit, year by year. The village was small. All the eligible men her age had already married. Anna was an old maid. Thus she let herself grow old and undesirable before her time, to lighten the burden of rejection.

One morning, as we stood waiting for cigarettes, Anna was given a large envelope to weigh. She did this with her usual sighs of distress and weariness, as if she were a beast of burden whose owner had piled yet another stack of wood on her groaning back. But an odd thing happened as she took the required stamps from the drawer and began to paste them onto the envelope. This was an airmail special and needed many stamps. And Anna discovered the possibility of making a whimsical design on the envelope with the bright, pretty squares. She giggled and pointed to what she was doing, her vast bosom heaving with pleasure. The stamps made the picture of a little house and the special delivery stamp went on top for a chimney, with enough stamps for a side wall. Anna was laughing with excitement now, her eyes black as raisins in the great pasty spread of her face. There was something appealing in her good humor, her sense of importance. She waddled into the back room to show her handiwork to her aged mother. Customers began to smile. Anna was pleased, then embarrassed, then sullen. Sighing, she slumped back into her chair. She took the money for the stamps, made change. The excitement was gone from her face and eyes. Yet from that brief moment we knew that Anna must have been very appealing as a young girl, her eyes bright and hopeful before the limitations of village life closed around her like a gray wall.

«««««« »»»»»»

"The people on the road from Valencia": Sometimes the brightest memories do not have names at all, just faces and warm hearts. It happened to be a blistering July day when the fan belt on our car broke on the road inland from Valencia. Even the busiest of Spanish roads are not dotted with garages and service stations as in the United States—and this was a small byroad in a mountain area. We knew that two of us—the women—would have to stay with the car while the men hitchhiked the many winding

miles back to Valencia. As they flagged down an old truck, we waved them off and then settled on the dusty roadside grass to wait.

Behind us rose the short, craggy mountains, brown with the burned fuzz of summer. Nothing moved, nothing sounded except a sighing wind in the olive trees and the distant hum of insects. Suddenly, almost out of nowhere, a man stood above us. A Spaniard? Yes, his speech showed he was Spanish but his appearance was nontypical—a short, stocky blond man, almost bald, with a soft, round face and rimless eyeglasses. He was up in his summer home, he told us, just behind the first hill. He had seen our trouble and came to help. Would we honor him with a visit to the house? One of his sons could be sent to watch the car.

The house was a primitive two-story structure of plastered stone, with designed tile floors, simple furniture, no screens—and a harried wife with six small children. It was better here for his family, the man explained; the summer heat of Valencian streets and a small, crowded apartment were too much for children. We guests were given cane-bottomed chairs, cold water in clay mugs and "the hospitality of his house." The wife hung shyly around the doorway; the children were sent scurrying out to play. We stayed there five hours, cool, sheltered, welcomed and entertained.

"I am a poor man," our host explained. "I am only a bookkeeper, but how lucky I am to have this house to offer you today."

At lunch, we all sat together along rough planks

set on trestles. For lack of chairs, several children stood, their little chins just above the table. As a cook myself, I knew how nervously (and generously) lunch had been stretched to include two unexpected guests. Our main dish was a steaming, yellowish soup. It had originally been the Family's Sunday dinner of chicken with vegetables and saffron rice; added hot water made full bowls all round. As a special treat, each adult was given a raw egg, cracked right into the hot soup. Our host joyously brought out a bottle of raw, white wine, cooled in the cellar and plugged with fresh leaves. Dessert was a basket of fresh, soft figs, still sun-warm and dusty from the trees by the roadside.

Warmed by their own hospitality, the family relaxed. The husband told jokes and his wife patted his cheeks out of sheer affection. The youngest child began to fret sleepily and was allowed to doze off right on the cool tiles of the floor. Two of the older girls danced *flamenco* and sang folk songs with a pre-adolescent lisp. Our host then brought out an old, hand-winding victrola and gave us a concert of squeaky love songs, sung in French. The hot afternoon wore on until the plastered stone walls began to give off an early evening coolness. We felt wonderfully isolated, detached—and at home. Then, over the lilt of a French soprano, came the sound of our car horn. The men were back from Valencia.

How could we say good-by, how could we thank our hosts enough for sheltering us on this long afternoon? The man of the house smiled, bowed and shrugged, his glasses misting over with the emotion of parting.

"Do this for me, please," he said solemnly. "Send me some magazines from your country. I cannot read the words but we can all look at the pictures. We have had the humble pleasure of showing you our life. Let us see how you live. Then we can be even better friends."

That was some time ago. We sent the magazines and have since lost the slip of paper with the man's name and address. Was it Pepe, Enrique, Fernando? Perhaps it was Juanito. The name is lost but every feature of his kind face stays very clear.

«««««« »»»»»»»

Paco Antonio Baez: Paco is tall and handsome in the proper Spanish tradition, with wavy, black hair, bright, expressive eyes and sternly cut features that are relieved by his cheerful, innocent smile. He is a fashion plate, the Beau Brummel of a tiny fishing village, with dark, well-cut suits, white shirts and silk ties, shoes with toes pointed in the Italian style and hair glossy with sweet, oily lotions.

Many Spaniards have been bypassed by the increasing prosperity of Spain. Their lives are as hard as ever, the sea as cold and stingy with its fish, the land as rocky and jealous of its fruits, the burdens heavy and the weather treacherous to a poorly-fed man in patched clothes who lives with his family in a one-room, unheated and unlighted cabin on the beach. But Paco, now twenty-four, was one of those who caught a good grip on the tourist boom that swept through his village.

He got work in a souvenir shop and studied English. "Me speak now," he will preface his comments, and then go on with "I say him" and "He speak me." But, despite these grammatical flaws, he stubbornly pursues his goal of communicating in English. He is determined to learn.

From a two-room apartment above a milk shop, which he shares with his parents, Paco appears each morning in pressed suit, snowy linen and glistening, carefully-combed hair. After some time, he left the souvenir shop and went to work in a small bar-cafe. Eventually, through determined labor, he became a partner. And when the bar expanded into a night club, with a band and snappily dressed waiters, Paco went along with it, a full-fledged businessman now. He still lives with his parents. He is still a smiling guest or solemn godparent when his relatives' babies are baptized in the village church. But he is now aware, and pleased to know, that the world is a big place. He is saving his money for a trip to Madrid, then a quick flying trip to London. "Me go moon maybe," he says, his handsome face alight with good fortune, his laugh ringing with confidence.

But beneath, Paco is still a boy of the village. He has no intention of ever leaving his own people for long. He wants a Spanish wife, a family, a place in the profession of villagers who saunter through their little town on Sunday evenings, bowing properly and courteously to friends and neighbors, and, above all, he wants to continue living in the close warp of relatives and family that binds all Spanish life together.

<<<<<<<<<< >>>>>>>>>>

"Tia": In Spanish, the word "tía" means "Aunt," and this special skinny, brown-faced little lady was known as "Tia, the bread lady" all through the countryside. Tia (who did, in fact, have many nieces working as maids in the bigger houses) was as inevitable as sunrise, as faithful as morning. Her home was in a large town, about seven miles away, but every dawn she boarded an early bus and, by breakfast time, she had visited the back door of a dozen customers in the far suburbs, carrying a broad, deep basket loaded with fresh bread, rolls and sweet cakes. All deliveries were made on foot and Tia's black-garbed body was bent almost double as she rushed along the main road and up the rocky pathways leading to the villas. She was infallibly good-natured, with gray hair drawn into a neat bun, blue eyes bright and tight, fine skin weathered as brown as a fisherman's.

For many little housemaids and cooks of the area, Tia was more than a "bread lady"; she was a walking newspaper, full of the news of town, and a trusted friend and reliable messenger. A message given to Tia by some love-struck niece at breakfast would be delivered by noon to a young man hoeing a garden villa three miles away. Tia worked around the year, every day except Sunday in the blazing summer sun, she tied a floppy hat over her gray hair; in the winds of winter a little black sweater covered her thin shoulders. Everyone knew her; even the priest in the village, the postman, the tourists called her "Tia." At the end of the day there would always be a few sweet crumbs left in her basket to give to the little children who crowded at the bus stop.

We had known Tia for some months before we realized that there was also a "tío" or Uncle. While Tia took the high roads to the villas, Tio, her husband, took the low road along the beach and through the cafes. His basket held peanuts, oranges, bananas and some packages of black-tobaccoed cigarettes. "Yes, he is my husband," Tia said proudly. "We have always worked together. Our five children are all in school. The oldest is studying to be a dentist, the youngest is just starting with the nuns."

One dusky evening, driving into the village, our headlights picked out two figures, walking toward the bus stop. The figures were slight, moving slowly, each with a big basket on the outer arm. They held hands, swinging their arms as they walked, like two lovers out for a stroll. The high road and the low road had met at the end of the day to go home together. It was Tio and Tia, his bread lady.

«««««« »»»»»»

Señor Don Miguel Gomez: Here is a keen, resourceful entrepreneur, typical of the energetic, educated Spaniard who is helping to meet his country's current problems head on. The *Señor* is formidably equipped for his work; he speaks English and French as well as his own language, is a chef in the grand tradition, knows horses, sherries, golf and sailing and, moreover, is charming, unhurried and diplomatic. Presently, he is part of a group building and developing resort areas in Spain. Señor Gomez is a realist. Unlike a certain class of privileged Spaniards, he does not resent the furious changes that are occurring in Spain. The American air bases, the throngs of tourists, the inflation and the "progress" which adds a helter-skelter tone to the formerly serene Spanish scene—the *Señor* accepts all this as the conditions of life, nothing more, nothing less.

He says, "It's all very well to be sentimental about what is happening to certain old and picturesque villages. They were—in a sense—lovely and peaceful. Wealthy Spaniards enjoy sitting on the terraces of their villas and smiling down on the peasants and the burros going about the slow and graceful rounds of village life. But it is like yearning for medieval castles and liveried servants to tend the great noblemen. It is passing, it *has* passed. We live in a world of gasoline and oil, of machines and functional architecture. These satisfy the demands of the people. They are here to stay. And Spain—as other countries—must come to terms with them. As a businessman, I must help my country grow up."

At sixty-five, Señor Gomez is powered with fine energy and ambition. He is building a golf course and hotel in one town, a new apartment building in another; his interests range from electrical development to more intelligent planning for growth of farm communities. He believes a Royalty will be re-established in Spain. He believes the transition will be peaceful. Politics, as such, do not concern him; he feels that working with and for the people—and for himself—makes more sense in the present exciting world. If you met him—or a Spaniard of his type—you would sense an energy and enthusiasm that is like a bolt of electricity. He is the descendant of sailors and soldiers who took the Spanish language and culture throughout the civilized world. He is a *conquistador* of boom.

««««««« »»»»»»»

Manolo Seguro: That is his true name and you can hear it echoing out, punctuated with cheers and *oles,* in all the major bull rings in Spain. Manolo is a brave and successful bullfighter from Malaga, young, agile, handsome and good-natured. In his home town, he is a much-loved hero, recognized everywhere he goes, sought after for *fiestas,* trailed through the streets by adulatory urchins and dreamed about by enraptured—though carefully chaperoned—*señoritas* who know him only as the tiny, gilt-garbed figure in the center of the arena. As a matador, he is skillful, courageous, poised and capable of superb control.

Out of the ring, Manolo is mild-mannered but alert, his eyes bright, his mouth quick to smile. We know him well and have spent many quiet evenings with him as he listened and laughed or chatted quietly, full of humor. His courtesy and elegant good manners never leave him. The cries of praise he has heard a thousand times in the Plazas de Toros do not seem to re-echo in his ears. He is a warm, friendly and modest young man.

This young bullfighter enjoys Americans and things American. He is a good dancer and once startled older *aficionados* in the Plaza by doing a few rock-and-roll steps as he caped the bull in the center of the ring. One night he was a party guest at the home of married American friends who were entertaining a visiting aunt. The aunt—Mrs. L.— was thrilled to meet a real bullfighter. Manolo showed his usual good-natured poise and listened attentively as the woman chattered to him in English about *her* life, *her* trip, *her* country. At one point in the evening, she remarked to her niece that "He's a nice young man. It's a pity that . . ." The noise of the guests drowned out her last words. When Manolo left, Mrs. L. confided that she was going to give the bullfighter some lessons tomorrow. The hour was late, the hostess tired. She asked no questions. She presumed her aunt was going to try to teach Manolo Seguro a little English.

Around nine the next morning, while still in her robe, the hostess heard voices in her living room. She opened the door a crack. To her horror, she saw this scene: A small table was set with silverware and crystal for two. Mrs. L., with the strident tones of a gym teacher on a hockey field, was showing Manolo Seguro how to open the front door, advance with hand out-stretched and say, "How *do* you do?" Manolo watched her seriously, did as she suggested and repeated the performance several times to please her.

Next, the aunt seated herself at the table, unfurled her napkin and signaled for Manolo to sit down. He smiled, bowed and took a chair. The lessons continued—hold the fork this way, break bread before eating, never leave spoon in cup, do not talk with the mouth full—basic, high-chair training in table manners. Behind the door, Manolo's friend felt a sweep of panic—and then smiled. Manolo would not fail her. This was a man whose poise and grace had held thousands enthralled, this was a man whose courtesy and good breeding were as familiar to Spaniards as his bravery. Her aunt had decided that, as a "foreigner," he must need lessons in simple etiquette. But Manolo would understand. And he did. His natural courtesy helped him through the two-hour lesson with the same poise he showed in the Plaza de Toros. It was natural for him. He could not show rudeness to a visitor to his country; he could not allow an older woman to feel awkward or unmannerly about him. In fact, he even said "thank you."

《《《《《《《《 》》》》》》》》

This is just a quick flip through a crowded album. Here a memory-picture of a shabby, teen-aged shepherd boy, standing alone on a hilltop, his gunny-sacking topcoat stained with rain; a gypsy child dancing naked beside a wagon on a cool, early morning; honeymooning army officers walking through the streets of the Canary Islands, impeccable in white uniforms, pastel little wives walking proudly at their sides. Each single figure, each person and his story fits as a bit of mosaic into the bigger picture of Spain today.

Chapter IX

MOSQUES, MOORS—AND OTHER MEMORIES

The day was brightly sunny but the wind off the Mediterranean was brisk and chill. The traditionally blue waters of the sea were scudded with whitecaps and the force of the undertow muddied the waves along the shore line. Even the tiny blue iris that pop up everywhere in Spanish springtime were brushed flat with the gale. We picked up our lunch basket, bent against the wind and climbed a steep hill to the round, crumbling tower at the top.

Inside, the tower was open to the sky, the thick grass of the old floor was strewn with tumbled brown rocks. Two grazing sheep stared at us and ambled out the broken, open doorway. We spread out lunch, seated in the almost silent pocket of ruins, protected from the wind that sang high overhead.

From this vantage point, we could look great distances up and down the coast line and far out over the wild sea, off into the faded horizon where the

Mosques, Moors—and Other Memories · 141

waters stretched on and on to Africa. We sat and stared, just as Moorish soldiers had kept watch in this tower centuries before us.

This was the ruins of a Moorish watchtower, built hundreds of years ago, when the Moors ruled much of Spain. It is one of many that still dot the jagged sweeps and curves of the Mediterranean coast, each one just barely visible from the last, in an unbroken signal line to alert against danger from land or sea.

In the old days, these towers were garrisons with sharp-eyed Moorish troops on constant watch. In time of danger, great oil flares were set afire on top of each tower, and the warning flames were picked up along the many-miled coast until every tower showed its signal and the whole populace was alerted. Because of the curves of the coast and the height of the hills, each flare could be seen for miles.

We happened to use that tower as a special picnic grounds; for the sheep it was a good pasture place, where grass grew thicker; sometimes gypsies set up camp within the walls. But these towers are familiar sights in southern Spain, so familiar, in fact, that they are no more astonishing to the eye than the hills or the sea itself.

In all Spain, the long, dramatic history of the country is woven in and out of the plainer pattern of modern living, touching it with color and splendor.

《《《《《《《《 》》》》》》》》

The legend of how the Moors from Africa swept into Spain and occupied much of its land for centuries seems typically Spanish—emotional, violent and touched with treachery. The story is that Count Julian, the Spanish governor of Ceuta, a city in northern Africa, had sent his young and beautiful daughter to Toledo to be educated there in the court of one of the Kings, Roderick. Some time later, the young girl smuggled a message down to her father to say that she had been sullied by the King in a fashion most unbecoming to a Spanish gentleman. In revenge, Count Julian allowed a Moorish scouting party to land in Spain, make plans —and invade successfully one year later.

This was in the early 700's, and for the next seven years, the Moorish forces crept upward, conquering province after province, until all but the north of Spain was in their possession. To the Spanish, they brought their laws, customs and civilization and ruled for seven centuries—until they, in turn, were forced back to Africa by the Christians, under Ferdinand and Isabella.

In many ways, the Moors never totally left Spain. Especially in the south, the dark hair and eyes, the passionate protection of women and the fiery pride of men seem a heritage of the Moors. And today many Spanish cities are still as Moorish in architecture as parts of Morocco itself.

In Seville or Cordoba, for instance, one walks through tiny, crooked streets, passing the high, blank white walls of houses and glimpsing only through a

Mosques, Moors—and Other Memories · 143

rare window or iron gate the elaborate courtyards, gardens and family arrangements within. The colorful tile floors and the mosaics that reach halfway up the courtyard walls, all open to the skies, are copied directly from the gardens of the Moors. The potted green plants or flaming geraniums that surround a tiny, tinkling fountain date back to the day when the Arabs were wandering tribes in the upper deserts of Africa, when water was life itself and a man of wealth liked near him the reassuring sound of gurgling springs. Even the climate here seems especially Moorish, since Cordoba and Seville swelter more in the summer months than other cities of Spain.

In Cordoba stands the famous mosque, now used as a Catholic church, but so Moorish and distinctive in its architecture that Allah might well still be honored within. The mosque was built in the eighth century and sits now in a spreading garden of fragrant orange trees, each plant clipped and groomed until it is as plumply rounded as the oranges themselves. The mosque is maintained inside by a breathtaking forest of red and white jasper columns, 850 in all, supporting a series of curved arches so constructed that one sees in every direction a perfection of symmetry and precision. In theory, the interior of a mosque should be built to bring calm for reflection; when the eye is pleased it can then turn inward and contemplate the soul. At first glance, the cool interior of this mosque looks like a superstructure of peppermint candy; a longer look shows the excellence of the planning. It is truly "peace through perfection." Here is one of the most beautiful heritages the invading Moors left to Spain.

In the mountain town of Ronda, too, the Moors have left their traces. We traveled there first on a bleak winter day, when the winds were high and the rains torrential. The long, twisting highway upward from the coast was clogged with boulders and the precipice side of the road yawned downward into pine-covered valleys, so deep we saw only the tops of the trees. One could not help envisioning the struggling Arab mule trains that wound their way up to Ronda when even this treacherous road did not exist.

In spite of the driving rain, we found eager guides crowding the streets, urging us to see the sights. One of the famous ruins is the well-preserved remains of a Moorish palace, colorfully tiled, gracefully arched and cold as death that day, with spectacular, slim balconies opening over the Guadiaro River. This abrupt river chasm is 530 feet deep and about 330 feet wide; over one portion of it stands a most impressive ruin—"the old bridge." In the old bridge is preserved the cooperative work of masons spanning several centuries; first, there is evident the work of the old Romans, then the Moors and then the ancient Spanish. It is considered one of the architectural curiosities of the world and is visited faithfully by all students of engineering who pass this way.

Mosques, Moors—and Other Memories · 145

In the town of Ronda itself, there are the usual appurtenances of the twentieth century—drugstores, cafes for hot chocolate, a couple of movie theatres—but our few bleak minutes spent examining the bridge over the gorge, wet through with rain, seemed to turn history back for centuries.

«««««««« »»»»»»»»

In all Spain (and perhaps in all the Moorish world), there is no more beautiful relic or example of Moorish architecture than the Alhambra, in the hill city of Granada. This famous palace-fortress was built by the Moors in the thirteenth and fourteenth centuries and took more than a hundred years to construct. Some say the name "Alhambra" comes from an Arabic word suggesting "red"—and much of the building *is* done in a fine, reddish brick; others say the "red" refers to the giant, blazing torches under which nightwork was done through the years of painstaking labor. Much of the Alhambra still stands and is in good repair; but much was destroyed, carted away or "built over" by Christians in the years that followed the fall of the Moorish kingdom in 1492.

What stands today is not impressive for its bulk or majestic sweeps (in fact, the first impression is one of "smallness") but for its delicate grace, beauty and craftsmanship. The park around the buildings was once planted by the Moors with myrtle, oranges and roses; now it blooms chiefly with grass and wild flowers. Just below the Alhambra there is a deep gorge, cut through by the noisy, rapid river Daro. From the hills on which it is located, the palace overlooks the city of Granada and the countryside. The characteristic peaked-arch windows of the building make delicate frames for the spectacular scenery beyond. One may see orange trees in delicate pastel bloom in the foreground, backed up by blue-gray mountains capped with snow.

We visited the Alhambra many times, first following well-informed guides, then wandering around by ourselves, to reabsorb the beauty. One of the most famous features of the remaining structures is the Hall of the Abencerrages, a perfectly square room with a lofty dome, all decorated in blue, red, gold and brown and edged by delicately trellised windows. It is here, according to legend, that Boabdil, the last king of Granada, prepared a great banquet for his chiefs—and then had them massacred on the spot. Spanish guides still point to a few dingy spots on the floor that are supposedly stains of chieftain blood. (I like especially another story about Boabdil: he is said to have fled Granada with his mother and an entourage after this last stronghold had been recaptured by the Spaniards. The party stopped on a distant hill, to gaze back at the beauty of Granada and the Alhambra and the great Boabdil broke into tears. His mother looked on with scorn and said, "Do not weep like a woman for something you could not hold as a man!")

The Court of the Lions is also famous for its beauty. It is a long, oblong area surrounded by a low gallery supported by 124 white marble columns.

The courtyard and part of the walls are covered with yellow and blue tiles and the whole is centered by a white alabaster pool, guarded by twelve white marble lions, symbolic of courage and strength.

There are many other rooms, walls, courtyards and pools but we were particularly interested in the bathing quarters on a lower floor. Here stand excellent remains of deep stone bathtubs, with plumbing arrangements for hot and cold water and openings for perfume or scent sprays to spout out after the water cleansings. Adjoining the baths are elegant chambers in which Moorish princes once entertained the women of their harems; above these rooms runs a narrow balcony, once used by musicians—deliberately blinded—who played music for the lovers below, whom they could not see.

Washington Irving, the well-known American author, was our Ambassador to Spain around 1830 and lived for a time in the Alhambra. His book, *Tales of the Alhambra,* gives an excellent reporter's picture of the place in those days (gypsies fed him dinner in the trash-littered courtyard) and the rough surrounding countryside. He always weaves some wonderful fantasies about what may or may not have happened in the peaceful days when the Alhambra was a haven for royalty, orange blossom fragrances and the sons of the nightingales. And it is no fantasy, of course, to remember that it was in the splendor of the Alhambra that Queen Isabella finally gave her royal blessing for Christopher Columbus' voyage to the New World.

Even with the constant stream of tourists that

pours through the old buildings, the peace and serenity that comes both from the architecture and the beauty of the countryside still pervades the old palace. Again, the Moorish grace, careful workmanship and the effects of skillful repetition soothe the spirit and awake the dreamers.

So famous is the Alhambra that it is a "must" on every tourist's list, but, unfortunately, some tourists approach its splendors with as little interest or reverence as they might display on buying a book of tickets for a romp through Disneyland. One particularly mellow spring day, we stood beside a great, still pool in a courtyard, watching the reflected arches of a colonnade as they shimmered in the clear blue water. A tourist child, about eight, began to peel an orange, carefully tossing the bits of rind into the pool. His mother, leaning against an ancient arch for a relaxing cigarette, called out brightly, "Don't fall in, darling!" In the old days, a Moorish guard might have stepped briskly from the shadows and cut off the child's head for such desecration. Watching the orange peels float on the water, such a punishment seemed just right for the crime!

<<<<<<<<< >>>>>>>>>

Even though centuries have passed since Spaniards regained control of their own country, Moors and things Moorish still permeate Spanish life in unexpected ways. For instance, even today, there are a few remote hill towns, isolated from modern life by distance and difficult terrain, where Spanish women wear veils in the old Moorish fashion, and there is one primitive area above Almeria where life is still lived much as the country Moors once lived it, with women tending flocks and doing most of the field work, while the men simply stay at home and are treated as "men."

Over and over again, we heard this particular illogical but curious anti-Moorish prejudice: the Moors accepted defeat and the loss of Spain bitterly and are still determined to come back, say some present-day Spaniards. All over Morocco, relatives of the long-vanquished Moors still hold the keys to homes and business places in Seville, Malaga, Cordoba and Granada. Should the enemy sweep back over the sea in this twentieth century, it would be an easy matter to turn their keys in the selfsame doors—and take over. How those keys (if they existed) would creak and twist in rusty locks, after nearly five hundred years without use!

Today, particularly in the robust southern areas, maledictions against the Moors are still a common part of peasant speech. The enemy is still the enemy. A farmer berating a balky mule, a cab driver who misses a green light, a fisherman pulling against rough waves—all might shout out harsh curses against the Moors.

A close woman friend of mine who lives on the Mediterranean coast told me that she was once almost engaged to a Moslem prince. The man came frequently to Spain on business. He was a family friend and was welcomed in the home—until her parents learned she was in love. All this happened just about fifteen years ago. My *señora* was forbidden to see her prince again. Was it because of religious differences? No, she said, the young man loved her enough to make a promise almost unheard of for a Moslem: he agreed to take instructions in the Catholic faith and to raise any children in that religion. Then why had her family objected so strongly? She shrugged and laughed ruefully. "He was a Moor, you know, and one just does not marry one of the enemy."

I heard, too, this variation of the "Moor myth," told about the little town of San Cruz del Retamar and its troubles. In this town of 4000 people, there are four hundred eligible bachelors and only about one hundred unmarried girls. For as long as the oldest townsfolk can remember, male babies have always outnumbered female babies here about three to one. The situation of life and love has become so tense that outsiders (boys from neighboring villages) must pay a 500-*pesetas* fee to court a San Cruz girl!

And how did this imbalance of the sexes come about? Centuries ago, so the story goes, when the area was still part of a Moorish kingdom, a Moslem nobleman fell from his horse and was badly injured. A Spanish Christian farmer rescued him and nursed him back to health. When it came time to part, the farmer called out an old Spanish farewell, "Go with God!"

The Moslem nobleman answered, "Since I am not of your faith, I cannot reply in kind but I *can* give you this wish: may your descendants be blessed with sons as numerous as the hairs of your head."

That was many hundreds of years ago, but the Moorish blessing (or curse?) is still believed to overshadow the love life of San Cruz del Retamar.

Of course, such memories and prejudices are two-sided and the Moors took a few dark thoughts back with them across the Mediterranean. It is only in the last ten years that devout Moslems have dropped from their regular evening prayers a plea to Allah to "restore to us Granada"!

<<<<<<<<< >>>>>>>>>

The ancient Roman conquerors, too, have left their majestic traces over the entire face of Spain. Roman domination lasted from about 200 B.C. to 300 A.D., a five-hundred-year span in which the Romans unified the fierce tribes of the country (then called Hispania or Iberia) and penetrated the entire vast wilderness with their administration, laws and building. At that time, Spain had 829 cities and excellent public works. The Romans were the first to try road-building through the difficult countryside and they constructed aqueducts, sewer systems and arenas which are still in evidence today.

Near Segovia stands an impressive Roman aqueduct with one-hundred-eight arches built from huge blocks of granite from the nearby Guadarrama mountains and still in working condition today. In western Spain, at the town of Meridia which once garrisoned 90,000 Roman legionnaires, are remains of a city-circling wall, a bridge and an amphitheatre. Other lesser ruins and traces of old Roman cities have been excavated all over Spain.

The major ruins are, of course, nationally important as historical triumphs and as tourist attractions but the many "little ruins" throughout the country are considered routine parts of Spanish life and landscape, little noticed by anyone. In the center of Malaga, I remember, there is part of an old Roman wall, plus a few broken pillars and assorted stones, all considered too incomplete for major interest. The city fathers have kept the area neatly grassed, with a bright flower or two preening itself against the weathered wall. This is a favorite spot for *novias* and *novios* to be photographed together but for sentimental rather than historical reasons. Most *Malagueños* regard the ruins with a "so what else is new?" casualness and indifference. Only stray cats seem to treat the wall and pillars with consistent interest. There are always several fat, appreciative felines stretched out in sleepy content. Perhaps the sun of centuries has truly warmed the old stones.

≪≪≪≪≪≪≪ ≫≫≫≫≫≫≫

In this century-flipping tour, let's turn the years back drastically until about 2000 B.C. Spain has its relics of that era, too, although sometimes they are presented to modern-day visitors as casually as a public drinking fountain. No signs, no fanfare. Just "there it is. Help yourself if you want."

Our discovery of one of Spain's most important

historic treasures came because we took the wrong road. We had driven to the town of Antequera, to try to buy a carved door. Many times we had stopped in this lovely old city with its big, chalk-white houses, each one with an exquisite front door. Some are carved with roosters, some are made of raised, tooled squares, some are studded with heavy iron, others glisten dully with shined old brass. We hoped to buy a door to be shipped back to America. *This*, we thought, is what is special about Antequera.

After stopping at one workshop and another, we were given directions to the studio of a master craftsman but we made a right turn at the wrong time—and shot right out of town. A narrow, grassed-over country lane looked like a good place to turn the car. As we entered, a one-armed man in a gray cotton civil service uniform rose from the stone on which he rested and signaled us on. We were expected.

Here at the end of the short lane was a "dolmen," a piece of prehistoric architecture so famous that it is known to archeologists all over the world. The guide lit a flashlight and we went inside. It is a post-and-lintel construction, meant to stand for all time—and this one is believed to date to 2000 B.C. These buildings were intended to be used as tombs and the dolmen at Antequera is about seventy-five feet long and more than fifteen feet wide, the whole set into the earth like a perfectly symmetrical cave, with the ceiling-stone roofed over on the outside with earth and grass. Inside, the walls, ceilings and floor were impressive single slabs of stone, huge and bafflingly big to have been cut and hauled by man. There are no remains, no relics here—just the structure itself, smoothed over with moss and wonderfully cool on that hot day.

The guide was one-armed, I mentioned, his empty sleeve tucked neatly in a pocket. It is a practice in Spain to award blind people or people with badly damaged sight the privilege of selling lottery tickets in the streets; and men crippled or incapacitated in the Civil War are given civil service jobs whenever possible. Our guide was one of these, showing tourists a national relic. He knew next to nothing about the prehistoric tomb itself, except that "many strangers like to stop here." But he laid his flashlight on the grass and we had a cool cigarette together, light from our matches making little glows on the ancient ceiling. And he told us all about *his* history and how he lost his arm in guerilla fighting in the hills behind Antequera.

<<<<<<<<< >>>>>>>>>

Say to anyone in Spain *"Uno Bisonte, por favor"* and you will be offered a cigarette because *"bisonte"* means "buffalo" and that is the name and trademark of one of the most popular brands of cigarettes in the country. Each package is marked with a distinctive, sharp-lined and artistic sketch of a buffalo. Yet this piece of artwork, as familiar to the Spanish eye as our "cigarette camel" is to us, was first scratched on a cave wall in northern Spain in the Magdalenian

Mosques, Moors—and Other Memories · 155

period of history, dating somewhere from 30,000 B.C. to 10,000 B.C.

The great cave, an underground art gallery, is near the northern city of Altamira and was discovered by accident in the late nineteenth century. (A little child was picnicing with his father and their pet dog ran into a cave. In rescuing the dog, the father sighted the cave drawings).

These "caves of Altamira" house the most famous group of cave drawings in the world. The illustrated ceiling is over forty feet long and is closely packed with sketches of some twenty-five animals, mostly bison. It is believed that the pigments were applied in liquid form and the colors are red, black and an earth-tone. It is thought that perhaps this underground cave was once used as a kind of temple; perhaps prehistoric man made the sketches as a propitiating "gift to the gods" in some year when game and food was scarce. The atmospheric conditions of the cave have preserved the drawings in excellent line and color, showing modern man the type of animal which existed in the area so long ago and giving him a knowledge of his own forebears.

Thus even in such little ways as a cigarette package, Spain and its colorful, intricate history live intimately together.

Chapter X

DIARY WITHOUT DATES

C̲ADIZ: "A long four-hour ride to this famous old port town, an ancient city dating back to 1000 B.C., when it was founded by Phoenician sailors. Once one of the great ports of the world, it went into a decline when the Spaniards lost their American colonies and never recovered. A curving mountain road and then miles of flat salt mines, spotted with giant pyramids of drying salt—this is the product of the local salt-marshes and even the breeze smells briny.

"On the road we passed old, high-bodied cars, crowded with eight and ten men on their way to the soccer marches in Algeciras. One car was run on steam generated from a small coal-burning stove attached to the rear end. It was Sunday and, in the smaller villages, the candy stands were out in the streets and men and women chatted in doorways, warming in the thin February sun. A few miles out of Cadiz, we were flagged down by a stalled car; ten young men on the way to the soccer matches had run out of gas. We had neither a container nor hose to syphon gas from our car to theirs, so they pushed their automobile to the side of the road, shrugged philosophically and began the trek to Algeciras on foot.

"Cadiz itself, set on an isthmus with seas crashing on three sides, seemed prosperous and high-spirited. The hotel, *Francia y Paris*, stood in the center of town, right next to the great brown cathedral. It's an old, three-story hotel, built up from a central lobby, with balconies running around the hub of each floor, all topped by a giant, colored-glass skylight. The walls of the chill dining room are covered half-way up with bright blue and orange tiles, the ceilings tinkly with heavy crystal chandeliers—a curious mixture of Moorish and Victorian.

"The streets of the town are so narrow that they seem to run together at the ends of the blocks. Heavy grilled windows still fluttered with bits of colored paper and broken balloons from a town fiesta four days before.

"At night, certain streets are jammed with promenaders. Obviously, some blocks are more 'chic' for walking than others. Crowds poured along as if at a carnival. We stopped for dinner at about ten o'clock and ate *angulas* (eel spawn in hot oil), thick steaks with mushrooms and vegetables and some local wine. The dining room was so cold that we warmed our fingers over the sizzling oil of the first course before trying to hold forks.

"In the daytime, the city seems very white and Moorish, with a deep blue harbor, lined with rough, rusty freighters. Here palm trees grow, lush and tall, as one would imagine them flourishing in Africa. On Sunday afternoon, we stopped at a seaside restaurant, crowded with men playing cards and listening to the blare of the radio broadcast of the Cadiz-Algeciras soccer match. It was as tense as the last game of our World Series. The card-players nibbled at hot, fried squid or paused to slip a cold clam-on-the-shell into their mouths. Their favorite drinks were hot, black coffee or milky glasses of pernod mixed with water. There were no women in sight and the customers seemed very prosperous and at-home.

"In many Spanish towns, travelers are troubled by children or poor people begging for pesetas. But not in Cadiz. Even the guide who showed us through the cathedral refused a tip."

«««««« »»»»»»»

Gibraltar: "It was Easter Sunday morning, and we had just left the rocky promontory of Gibraltar, the fortress rock that is part of Spain but owned and maintained by the British. The sun was bright and the road gently twisting through spring-green hills. Good cigarettes are at a premium in Spain, and at Gilbraltar we had bought a carton of Pall Malls, now safely tucked in the glove compartment. On a curve of the road, we saw three very young Spanish infantrymen in coarse greenish uniforms, squatting in the grass. It was their day off but they obviously had no money to spend, nowhere to go.

"One waved at the car as we approached and made a hopeful gesture, putting two fingers to his lips as if he were smoking. We stopped a few yards further on, and the three boys came pounding down the road. Impetuously, we gave each soldier a fresh pack of cigarettes and matches. They thanked us but looked baffled with joy.

"A few moments later, we glanced in the rear vision mirror and saw the three soldiers, arms around each other's waists, skipping back down the road, heavy boots clumping and the little red tassel on each hat swinging in unison. They were like exaggerated, animated little figures from a Disney cartoon. I think we felt as happy as they did."

«««««« »»»»»»»

The Road to Valencia: "Taking the inland road from the southern coast up to Valencia on the east, the first miles were routinely beautiful, passing through mountains, then flat fields spotted red with poppies. About dusk, we stopped at the little town of Guadix and were immediately picked up by a 'runner' from the single hotel. He jogged in front of the car up a narrow, stoned street to the hotel. It was an aged place, with out-sized, drab furniture in the lobby, soiled lace antimacassars and rubber plants dying in their pots. Adjoining the lobby was the town's main cafe, a dark room with marble-topped tables crowded with men playing cards and checkers. These were middle-class businessmen, finishing their day with a game of cards and a bottle of wine. A dank fog of old cigar smoke and stale olive-oil hung over the room. We decided not to spend the night.

"At the edge of town, we stopped to buy a tall

white shepherd's crook and a thin brown can with a flexible stem. The stout old lady in black was very good-natured and wrote out all the prices clearly on paper, thinking we did not understand the local currency. Outside, a shabby urchin, heat pitted with ring-worm scars, approached us with a basket of peanuts. We bought half a dozen packages—just a few peanuts in twists of brown paper—for about five pesetas each, or sixty cents for the whole purchase. This was sheer robbery but the little boy seemed too undernourished and ill to argue with; perhaps his mother put an egg in his soup that night because he had had a prosperous day.

"Passed next through a 'cave town,' a little village of a hundred or more homes made from natural caves and artificial hollows scooped in the soft, low rocks. Most caves had wooden doors, painted light blue or white, occasional chimneys and even clumps of geraniums or little vegetable gardens planted in front. Laundry was spread out on the grassy roofs to dry and women gossiped in the doorways of their unlit homes as casually as women passing the time of day in a neighborhood market. We were told that such caves are considered blessings by poor Spaniards—cool in summer, easier to keep warm in winter and, naturally, no landlord to worry about."

<<<<<<<<< >>>>>>>>>

Murcia: "This old town was the next stop on our map, a city that also existed on the maps of the old Romans. The approaching scenery was startling, mostly low pink and green mountains, many in such repetitious perfection that they looked unreal. In fact, they seemed so soft and rounded they might have been pressed and stroked into shape by some giant hand. Next came areas of brown rock, rhythmically serrated like small sections of the Grand Canyon. No wonder a Spaniard from one province can feel like a stranger in another; no two parts of Spanish landscape look alike!

"About nine o'clock, we slowed down while passing through the little town of Velez Rubio (20,000 people live here, yet it seemed as quiet as a small village), and a waiter ran out of a restaurant to flag us down. Spain is not strung with Howard Johnson-type eating places like the United States but tiny cafes survive over the years with just a half-dozen diners per night. This restaurant was one big room, bewilderingly cluttered with potted plants, ornate water jugs and calendars with sugar-sweet pictures of saints. The menu was typical of such stopover-cafes, a lot of food and all of it mediocre. We began with lukewarm consomme and rice, a second course of artichokes, beans and neckbones all cooked in thin gravy, fried chicken and tough veal chops, lettuce and tomatoes and, for dessert, a thin slice of white, grainy goat's cheese and a slice of fruit jelly. This last is something which we don't have in the United States, a tough as-rubber jelly made of quinces, sugar and gelatin. It is considered a delicacy, especially good for children and invalids.

"There was one moment of drama in our stopover. A local girl was scheduled to sing a *flamenco* number on a radio amateur hour beamed from Murcia and, at the appointed hour, curious townspeople crowded into the restaurant to listen. Only her father seemed to be missing and the waiter whispered to us ominously, '*She is doing this against her father's wishes. To be an entertainer is to be a bad woman.*' But her father need not have worried. In the voting at the end of the show, 'the little star of Velez Rubio' did not even get honorable mention.

"Arrived at Murcia around midnight and found the town brightly awake, cafes crowded, streets honking with cab traffic. This is a prosperous town, set in mountains rich in various ores and with farmfields carefully irrigated with systems set up centuries ago by the Moors.

"In the morning, from Murcia up to Valencia, the scenery was hot, dusty and brilliant, very African. We passed through village after village of white houses set along red-dust roadways, with occasional buildings painted in chalky pink and blue. At one point, we drove through the famous towering date palm forest, planted by the Moors, with the trees still fruitful.

"As we finally approached Valencia, the irrigated fields stood out in brilliant pea-green precision. These were the rice fields, operated in strangely primitive fashion; here and there men walked through the watery rows in bare feet, sprinkling seed by hand; again we passed farmers ploughing behind horses, riding planks like surf boards over the irrigating waters. On a high hill, ending a twisting road, stood a perfect castle silhouetted against the sky. It had once belonged to the Borgias. Outside Valencia, the rich acres of orange groves spread fragrance and color. They were heavy with fruit. These highways, too, were heavy with truck traffic, a rarity in Spain. The country has some railroads and some trucking, of course, but, except near heavy industrial or rich farm areas, it is still the sure-footed little donkey that bears most of the burdens."

«««««« »»»»»»

Valencia: "This is one of the glamour cities of Spain, along with Seville, Barcelona, San Sebastian and Madrid. The city is divided into the old city—and the newer section that has expanded to make room for the half-million inhabitants. The great Cathedral of Valencia, incidentally, is built on the site of an old Moorish mosque, which, in turn, was built on the site of an Ancient Roman Temple of Diana!

"Shops sell expensive clothing, in-town boulevards are lined with blooming lilac, fountains spray in every square. Here there is an opera and theater season in the winter months, great homes stand behind high grilled fences and wealthy students go to study in London, ski in Switzerland or polish their French in Paris. This represents only a small portion of the people, of course, but in Valancia there *is* money and high-living.

"It was in here that we went to our first Spanish

dinner-dance, with dinner served promptly at midnight and the waltzing and tea-for-twoing going on to a giddy, orange blossom-scented dawn. The Valencians seem to take a joy in living from the lush, fertile fields and groves which surround them and make them privileged citizens in their own country."

Granada again: "The long road back, with field poppies, daisies and blue iris seeming to have multiplied by the thousands in the few days since we passed this way. Outside Granada, we stopped to rest and sat on the roadside in the moonlight; olive trees shown silver-green, there was a sweet scent of orange orchards, and from the valley, a sound of running water. Out of the darkness came the clop-clop of hoofs, then a donkey with a sleepy rider, faithfully taking his master home in the night. In the next stillness, we heard a special sound for the first time, yet it was so rare and so sweet we knew at once what it was. We were listening to nightingales singing!"

Coin: "Not a golden shiny-penny town as the lovely name suggests but another tucked-away mountain spot, white with houses, blue with mountains and brown with dust.

"Travelers see much of any country in a somewhat lonely fashion, looking for comfort and company in public places, such as cafes, town squares and restaurants. One cannot depend on overnight friendships—but watching and listening to people at the next table is one way of 'making friends.'

"We drove into Coin on a warm, moist spring Sunday. The little streets were crowded with couples, walking arm in arm, girls in threes or fours, arms linked, elaborately groomed in pastel dresses. Many carried missals and lacy head-scarves, showing they had come from the village church and late Benediction services.

"The village cafe was made up of three large, joining rooms, built around an open brick courtyard, heavy with vines, roses and giant calla lilies. The proprietor and his family, ranging from a toothless grandmother in rusty black to little boys under six, were seated at a long wooden table, chatting and sipping wine. At another table, an enormously plump young matron shared a bottle of vino with her husband in silence; two children sat quietly by, making dolls and designs out of flower petals. All were stiffly prim in their Sunday best.

"We took the next table and were served a saucerful of bread and sausage chunks, plus two bottles of *gaseosa*, a kind of thin, carbonated Spanish lemonade, good for both giving and curing the hiccups!

"In one corner of the cafe stood a pedestal, topped with a lace doily, holding a white clay water jug. Vendors came in, balancing baskets of sweet cakes, candies and peanuts on their heads; all stopped to drink from the jug in Spanish fashion, holding it high so a little arc of water spouted into their mouths without spilling a drop.

"Young men in clean, mended shirts sauntered in to stand at the bar. The parish priest seated himself at a table alone, nodding solemnly around the room; then he sipped coffee and read his breviary. A long, sharp-ribbed dog rose to sniff hopefully among the peanut shells on the floor. Outside, in the street, a troop of donkeys, loaded high with brushwood for cooking, tick-tacked along the cobblestones. A whiff of fresh, tangy balsam floated in through the doorway as they passed. Later, a herd of sheep trekked down from the mountain pasture and wandered through the town to their stables, the bell of the lead ewe sounding with a melancholy clank.

"The children with their flower petals gathered their fragile treasures and moved to our table to play. Both parents nodded at us and beamed with pride: we were indeed honored to be chosen by their offspring. Even on this warm spring night, the little girl wore her coat of brown and white rabbit skin, the height of fashion for small-town children. The proprietor's wife left her family and served us each a tiny cup of black coffee, heavy with sugar, compliments of the house. There was little noise in the cafe, just the tinkle of an occasional peseta on the bar, the gentle rise and fall of conversation and a feeling of resting. After all, it was Sunday in Coin."

<<<<<<<<< >>>>>>>>>

San Sebastian: "This lovely old city is the graceful, gray queen of the north. Though Spain is chiefly an agricultural country, all of its life is not rugged or rural. In fact, Spanish elegance at its height can make most of us feel like awkward, country cousins. San Sebastian is such a place, a resort city of about 150,000 people and just twelve miles from the French frontier. Here the streets are wide and clean, little nightclubs glitter, golf and tennis are easily available and the luxury shops are filled with fine silks, jewelry and leather goods. In summer, when tourists flock in from France and Spain, the air is always fresh and cooled by the breezes of the Bay of Biscay, bathing beaches are broad and fine-sanded. In winter, most of the expensive seaside hotels shutter against the brisk winds and hibernate behind their heavy velvet draperies until spring. A fine time to clean silver, shine crystal, plump feather mattresses and dust the intricate carved woods and satin brocades of the dining rooms, ballrooms and guest halls.

"It was a cold November night when we first stopped at San Sebastian. Perhaps we were cold, perhaps we were tired, but the luxury of the town seemed awesome. We picked the Hotel Londres, partially open for travelers, and were greeted by a uniformed doorman in the curved drive of the street side. All downstairs but the main lobby of the hotel was closed off for the winter; here the thick carpets added to the silence; dim lamps lit only small circles of luxurious comfort or shone on the white feet of marble statues and gilt-framed oil paintings. Our rooms opened on balconies overlooking the water, where waves crashed freezing spray along the broad promenade. Lines of decorative trees, trimmed and stunted until they looked like rows of giant cloves, were hoared with frost. The room itself was done in pale green brocade, rugs a soft, faded rose and with a marble bathroom big enough to scrub a family of six. Little maids came to draw the heavy draperies, light the fireplaces, warm the bathtowels, turn down the beds and slip in hot-water-bottles.

"We had dinner served in our room before the fire—excellent grilled trout, tender roastbeef, mushrooms brought in from France—all offered by white-gloved waiters against a background of roaring sea wind and crackling logs. Firelight flickered on the long walls of closets; not mere holes-in-the-wall in which to hang bikinis, sunsuits or sandy beach clothes, but vast, scented spaces meant to hold ball gowns, evening slippers, walking costumes, tennis dresses—the elegant summer wardrobes of Spanish *bon vivantes* and nobility some thirty years ago.

"San Sebastian is still a popular resort town, still the place where most officials of the current Spanish government choose to spend the summer months. But at one time it was the choice of royalty—and those who clustered around them—for vacations. After World War I and the fall of the monarchy, the luxurious gray city never recovered its royal position. It must have had a storybook grandeur in its heyday.

"We went to sleep that night with the roar of wind and waves solid outside the windows. But not a draft ruffled the draperies. Satin eiderdowns hugged around our shoulders and the fireplace logs flickered and stayed aglow until dawn. It must have been pleasant to have been a Spanish princess in the old days—or even a Spanish duchess!"

※※※※※※※※　※※※※※※※※

The Island of Ibiza: "We are taking an overnight boat ride from Valencia. Ibiza is the littlest island of Balearic group, much smaller than its sisters, Majorca and Minorca, yet big enough to have been put on sailors' charts as long ago as the Phoenicians.

"At night the blue Mediterranean seems as rough and ominous as any ocean. Most passengers slept on deck, bundled in overcoats, nibbling at cheese and oranges from their pockets. We shared a four-bunk cabin with two Spanish matrons. At bedtime, they slipped voluminous nightgowns over their heads and undressed beneath, using the gowns as "tent dressing rooms." By dawn, the Spanish island was in sight, painted against the horizon like a stage-drop, white houses and crooked streets climbing a main hill to the brown cathedral at the top.

"Time seems turned back here. Aside from the main town of Ibiza, only three or four other small villages dot the shores. There are few cars, mostly ancient taxis. Country roads jog with donkey-drawn wagons, their passengers—both men and women—sheltering themselves with black umbrellas against the fierce sun. In this remote area, women seem truly peasant in dress—black blouses, long, full black skirts and heavy hair worn in one plait swinging down the back. Young girls add a single, springy curl at each temple, a bit of hair curled around a heated nail. At *fiesta* time, a kind of shawl is added —a triangle of dull-colored velvet hung with fringe.

"Windmills pump water on Ibiza and horses thresh out wheat by treading on it in the fields. In mid-summer, whole areas glow bright, rich orange when the apricot crop is spread out to dry in the sun. Farming and fishing supply the meager livings. At dawn, scores of primitive boats shove off from shore, yet so rugged and lonely are parts of the coast that one can spend a whole day in an isolated cove without seeing a boat or another human being.

"Tiny country houses often stand lonely, shielded from the road by fences of spiky paddle cactus, their white-washed mud walls covered with blue morning glories. Little children run naked in the farmyard or share the stone-floored single room with chickens and geese.

"Village life seems equally simple. At night, a single radio from the cafe may entertain the whole town, a single light bulb illuminate the square. In the bright sun of morning, women gather about the town fountain to fill water jugs for the day or troop to the hills to pound family laundry in the brook and dry it on the sun-heated rocks. At nightfall, the teen-aged girls of each house sprinkle water around the doorstep and roadway, like farmers throwing grain to hens, to settle the dust of the day.

"There are Roman ruins here and Phoenician and Moorish and Ibiza itself seems barely part of the twentieth century. Yet these little islands, plus the Canaries and a bit of African desert, are all the outposts that are left to Spain whose great red and gold net of empire once stretched out to Africa, Mexico and the Americas."

Chapter XI

HASTA LUEGO, AMIGOS

Hasta luego means *farewell for the present* and most Spaniards prefer it to the more abrupt and final *adios* or *good-by*. And travelers, armchair or otherwise, also find a final farewell to Spain almost impossible. It is an intriguing country, challenging and filled with changes. Why say good-by—ever—when Spain will wait as it has for centuries to re-offer up its charms?

Any farewell has touches of sadness, sometimes for the things done, sometimes for the things left undone. In this book there are still so many things left *unsaid* that one can only hope that *you* will see Spain one day for yourself and fill in the gaps and memories.

For instance, how strange is the sight of the river gypsies who travel the curving coastal roads of Spain, trailing on foot or crowded as families into a rickety donkey-drawn cart. These nomad people wander today as they did through the centuries, without any affiliations except a fierce loyalty to their own freedom. A drying river bed or a rare roadside spring determines their home—for the night only. A fire

Hasta Luego, Amigos · 173

of twigs for cooking, a bit of food foraged from farmers or fishermen, a few hours of weaving river-reed baskets to sell in the next village—and then wandering on again, road after road, year after year. Ragged, dark-skinned, lean—but proud to be gypsies. This is Spain and these are Spaniards. Isn't there *more* here that one would want to see and know?

Or the elegant bar of the Palace Hotel in Madrid around cocktail time, seven to ten at night by Spanish hours. The white-gloved waiters, the chattering, well-dressed tourists, the distinguished Spanish businessmen sipping sherry and quietly reading the evening papers. All set against a background drama of exquisitely perfect Spanish girls, dressed like movie starlets in bright gowns and small furs. Hair is either deftly simple or coiffed in as many curls and swoops as an American show girl, make-up is heavy but expert, perfume lingering. Such a girl may make a calculatedly stunning entrance, usually accompanied by an older woman. Her hour or two will be spent sipping lemonade at a table of older people, men and women, smiling quietly, talking little, fussed over and petted. Who are these celebrities, these very special people? Just wealthy young Spanish girls, decked and displayed like flowers by their doting parents. Yet aside from this rare and well-chaperoned excursion, their lives are almost as protected and curtailed as though they lived in harems. Is one not curious to know even *more* about a country and society that lives by such customs?

Or a stone-poor mountain village when death

strikes and the village priest hurries through the streets, his black robes stirring up the dust. No undertaker here, just sadness and a hasty burial within twenty-four hours, the dead soul lying in state in his own bed in his own tiny room, the harshness of the scene solaced by candles and the droning prayers of black-garbed neighbors. And yet in the same house, on a day of joy such as a baptismal, friends will crowd to share a *carafe* of wine and a plate of sweet cakes and stay to dance until dawn on the cobblestoned street. Is there not much *more* to learn about a people who can experience such peaks and valleys of emotional life with such courage and pride—and with so few material aids?

And other sights and sounds of Spain—a triumphant bullfighter being carried shoulder-high through the streets after a successful *corrida;* Generalissimo Franco's mounted Moroccan guard, riding gilt-hoofed horses at big parades and state gatherings; the opera season on Madrid; the poets' contest in Barcelona where the third prize is a gold rose, the second prize a silver rose and first prize a single perfect *real* rose; and the miles of beach at sunset with fishermen mending their great tar-covered nets, patient spiders crawling over the webs spread out on the sand.

There is so much to see and hear and learn and love in Spain, that I am glad I must say only *hasta luego* to this country. It has claimed me as an old friend; it would welcome you as a new one.

INDEX

Algeciras, 156, 158
Alhambra, The, 78, 145-148
Altamira, 155
Antequera, 153

Balboa, Vasco Nunez de, 84
Balearic Islands, 169-171
Barcelona, 23, 24, 107, 163
Benalmadena, 17
Brandy, 16
Bullfighting, 105-125

Cadiz, 64, 110, 156-158
Cafes, 26-29
Carahuela, 1, 3, 4
Cartama, 45, 46
Casals, Pablo, 67-68
Cervantes, Miguel de, 72-73
Christmas, 58-60
Churriana, 43
Class distinction, 31, 92, 93, 104, 135
Coin, town of, 164, 165
Columbus, Christopher, 34, 77-79, 147
Conquistadors, 83-85

Cooking, 15-17
Cordoba, 142, 149
Cortes, Hernando, 84
Court of the Lions, 146
Courtship, 49-55

Dali, Salvador, 66

Education, 89, 90, 98, 99
El Escorial, 80
El Greco, 79, 80
Entertaining, 41, 42, 57

Fallas of San José, 40, 41
Ferdinand, King, 75, 76
Feria of Seville, 41
Fiestas, 4, 7, 33-48
First Holy Communion, 57, 58, 103
Food, 15-26, 28-32
Franco, Francisco, 68-70, 80, 89, 103

Gibraltar, 158
Goya, Francisco, 82, 83

175

176 - Index

Granada, 3, 34, 78, 146, 149, 164
Guadix, 159
Gypsies, 41, 98, 147, 172

Holy days, 33-41
Holy Week ceremonies, 34-40, 62
Home life, 8-14

Ibiza, Island of, 169, 170
Ignatius of Loyola, 73-75
Inquisition, 75-77
Isabella, Queen of Spain, 75-79, 147

Jews, 75-77

Madrid, 24, 79-82, 107, 163
Malaga, 8, 17, 34-36, 87, 90, 95, 96, 107, 149, 152
Manners, 13, 65, 138
Manolete, 70-72
Markets, 19-21
Mealtimes, 13, 23, 24
Mexico, 85, 108, 171
Middle Ages, 5, 75, 79
Moors, 2, 78, 140-151
Morton, H. V., 76
Moslems, 64, 75, 149, 150
Mourning, 61, 62
Murcia, 160, 162

Olive oil, 15-17
Olive trees, 18

Oranges, 19
Orange trees, 18

Paella, 31
Pamplona, 117, 118, 121
People, 2-10, 86-104
Philip II, 80, 81
Phoenician sailors, 156, 169
Picasso, Pablo, 67, 90
Piropo, 49-51
Prado Museum, 80

Religious ceremonies, 37, 57, 58
Rome, 108
Roman domination, 151, 152
Roman ruins, 1, 163, 170
Romeria, 47, 48
Ronda, 144
Ruins, 1, 151-155

St. John's Day, 63
Salamanca, University of, 84
San Cruz del Retamar, 150, 151
San Fermin, 117-119, 121
San Sebastian, 10, 163, 166-168
Segovia, 151
Semana Santa, 34-40
Seville, 41, 42, 85, 142, 149, 163
Sherry, 18
Shops, 19
Siesta, 26, 27
Sixtus IV, Pope, 76

Spanish Civil War, 10, 68-
    70, 89, 154
Stranger in Spain, 76

Tetuan, 64
Television, 92
Tio Pepe, 18
Toledo, 80, 126, 142
Torquemada, 74-77

Valencia, 10, 11, 18, 40, 128, 159, 162, 163

Valladolid, 75
Valpedenas, 18
Velazquez, 80-82
Velez Rubio, 161, 162
Virgin of Cartama, 44-46

Weddings, 55-57
Wines, 17, 18

Young People, types of, 86-104

MAUREEN DALY

was born in County Tyrone, Northern Ireland, and grew up in Fond du Lac, Wisconsin. She first won literary distinction when she was sixteen, with a short story called *Sixteen* which placed first in a national short story contest sponsored by *Scholastic* Magazine and was selected for the annual O. Henry Memorial Award volume. Her first novel, *Seventeenth Summer*, won the Dodd, Mead Intercollegiate Literary Fellowship contest and quickly became a best seller. She has never stopped writing since—writing vigorously, simply and always with a new appeal.

Her articles and short stories have appeared in many national magazines and, as a reporter-columnist for the *Chicago Tribune* and later as an Associate Editor of *Ladies' Home Journal*, Miss Daly toured throughout the entire United States, as well as foreign countries from Iceland to Italy to Nigeria, talking with and writing about people, their interests and their problems.

On each trip abroad, Miss Daly found time to visit Spain, touring from the Pyrenees to the southern Mediterranean, and finally established a second home there, outside of Malaga. With her husband, writer William McGivern, and two children, Megan and Patrick, Miss Daly now spends a part of each year in southern Spain.

Date Due

NOV 2 '77			
NOV 23 '77			
OCT 19			
OCT. 1 5 1985			
FE 14 '89			
DE 4 '90			
NO 23 '93			
DE 6 '93			
DE 21 '93			
JA 11 '95			
AP 10 97			

914.6
Dal   6097

Daly, Maureen

Spanish roundabout